CRACKING THE
HIDDEN JOB MARKET

CRACKING
THE HIDDEN
JOB MARKET

HOW TO FIND OPPORTUNITY
IN ANY ECONOMY

DONALD ASHER

TEN SPEED PRESS
Berkeley

This book is dedicated to my mother, Dr. Ruby Faye Asher Ausbrooks, who has battled four cancers and is still with us. Mom, you have been an inspiration every day of my life.

Published in the United States by Ten Speed Press, an imprint of the Crown Publishing Group, a division of Random House, Inc., New York.
www.crownpublishing.com
www.tenspeed.com

Ten Speed Press and the Ten Speed Press colophon are registered trademarks of Random House, Inc.

Library of Congress Cataloging-in-Publication Data

Asher, Donald.
  Cracking the hidden job market : how to find opportunity in any economy / Donald Asher. — 1st ed.
      p. cm.
  Includes index.
  1. Job hunting. 2. Success in business. 3. Career development. I. Title.
  HF5382.7.A836 2010
  650.14—dc22
                                    2010010857
ISBN 978-1-58008-494-9

Cover and interior design by Betsy Stromberg

First Edition

CONTENTS

ACKNOWLEDGMENTS

This book is based on twenty years of working with job seekers, from CEOs to college students. The handouts and instructional aids that support those lectures and workshops are one source for the material in this guide. They are used with permission of Asher Associates, 415-543-7130, www.donaldasher.com. All rights reserved.

Some sections of this book appeared in other forms in my earlier books, including *How to Get Any Job, The Foolproof Job-Search Workbook,* and *The Overnight Resume*. They are used here with permission of Ten Speed Press. All rights reserved.

I am indebted to Gerry Crispin, SPHR, and Mark Mehler of CareerXroads for permission to release selected data from their study, "Sources of Hire (2008): Why You Should Care About This Now: Current Data, Trends, Opportunities and Challenges for 2009." For more information about their annual study, contact CareerXroads at www.CareerXroads.com or 732-821-6652. Sections used here with permission of CareerXroads. All rights reserved.

All names have been changed in this book. All examples are based on real people and real events, but no example mentioned in this book should be assumed to be a particular person and any such assumption would be unwarranted.

PREFACE: HOW TO USE THIS BOOK

I wrote this book with a particular reader in mind. If you are smart, hard working, a real contributor, and someone who is open to new things, great! We're on the same page. My goal is to help good people find the employment that will advance their personal and professional objectives. I like to write for and advise intelligent people. Since most people don't read books, and you're reading this one, I'm just going to assume you're one of the good people: a high performer who wants to be of value to others and make the world a better place for all.

Most job seekers look for work this way: they try things out, see what seems to work and what doesn't, then revise their approach and go at the project again. In this book, important steps to the search are presented in the order in which you would normally begin doing them. But here's the problem: you've probably already started your job search. You don't have time to read this book from cover to cover before you get out there and try some of these approaches. So, recognizing that you're already in the thick of things, I have crafted an organizational structure that supplies information in more than one spot, often introduced in one place and then more fully explicated in a later chapter. So, be aware that information is in more than one section. Use the table of contents, the index, and a little common sense to get the most out of this guide. Skip any parts that don't apply to you, or that you find boring. Feel free to skip ahead. You can always return to these sections later if they become more relevant. In the real world, you learn as you go. You're going to do some things right and some things wrong. You may eventually decide to go back and do some things over from scratch. You will definitely decide to do many things *systematically* that you had been doing haphazardly.

I will put my disclaimer right here: this book is not for everybody. I will ask you to do things that most people don't like to do, such as contact strangers and ask for something. However, not liking something is relative. Do you dislike foreclosure? Do you dislike the idea of being unemployed for a long time? Do you disdain the idea of begging your parents and members of your family for just enough money to get through another month while you wait for a career miracle? If you can say to yourself, "Yes, some of the techniques make me feel uncomfortable, and feel a bit risky, but they definitely look like they're going to work," then this book is for you. If you look at some of the suggested approaches and say to yourself, "I'd rather beg on a street corner for my next meal," then pursue that option. There is logic to the hidden job market, and it is presented in this book. If this logic makes sense to you, so will the book. One thing is certain, however: continuing to do the same thing over and over again and expecting a different outcome is the definition of insanity.

This may not be the only job book you need. You'll probably need a resume book and an interview guide. You may need some reference works peculiar to your field. You should read a new career book about once a week during your job search. Check them out from the library or borrow them if you don't want to buy them. This book should be, however, *your central guide to getting a great new job*.

1

MUSICAL CHAIRS AND PORRIDGE

The Labor Economy

The labor market is like a cruel and heartless game of musical chairs. When the music stops, you'd better get your butt on a seat. The clever, the nimble, and the quick may find a chair. This book is about how to be clever, nimble, and quick.

In a good economy, about half of all jobs go to someone who did not respond to an advertisement of any kind. They had friends on the inside, or they walked up at the right time. In a bad economy, even more jobs go to insiders. Employers can have their choice of candidates—too much choice, in fact. I could post an ad for a redheaded, five-foot-tall, Australian trick pony rider, and get stacks of applicants. Almost all of them would be willing to ride a pony, and more than some of them would be redheaded, five feet tall, and Australian. Once a job is posted, you have to be perfect, you have to have friends on the inside, or you have to be the first in line. This book is about getting friends on the inside, or being at the head of the line.

I recently spoke with a Fortune 1000 HR manager who still gets a stack of paper resumes *every day*. He grabs a two-inch slice out of the pile every morning and throws away the rest. "I don't want to hire anyone who is unlucky," he says, "and there are only so many hours in the day." This book is about how to create your own luck.

What most people believe about a job search is wrong. By using the wrong techniques, you could look for work forever without finding employment. Or you could decide to learn something new, something radically different.

That's what this book is about. Something new and radically different. It's about understanding the invisible part of the job market, and learning how to get into that invisible world and play it to your advantage. The **hidden job market** is all the jobs that change hands without being advertised, and jobs that may be advertised but go to insiders. This book is about how to be an insider. To manage your career today you must understand this world. Let's start right now.

First, all industries are always hiring. Even when you read that an industry is imploding, it's hiring at the same time. When you read that a large company is laying off thousands of workers, it is almost always hiring some new people at the same time.

Now, to be fair, not all organizations will be hiring, but in all industries at all times, there is hiring. People die on the job and they need to be replaced. People decide to retire. They get injured. They go on maternity leave. Too many people take vacations at the same time, yet the work still has to get done. A department is downsized but the remaining workers don't have the exact right skill sets, so HR has to bring in a couple of people with specific talents. Even when a bankrupt government or company has a hiring freeze, it will have an exception process for "essential workers." The smarter large organizations hire new college grads *every year in any economy*, otherwise their idea flow would come to a screeching halt.

You cannot be an effective job seeker until you get this: all industries are hiring, right now, all around you. We'll talk later about how to identify growth, but that's not nearly as important as understanding that hiring goes on everywhere, all the time, even when companies and industries are contracting. You can't get lucky, or develop friends on the inside, or get there first, until you can *believe* that jobs are out there.

You get a job by talking to people. You don't get a job by having a great resume, a good interview look, a firm handshake, or a solid education. You get a job because you get in front of somebody, and she decides to add you to the payroll. You get to talk to employers by talking to *people*. Most job seekers look for jobs by talking to computer software. It's faster to talk to *people*. People are more likely to pass you along than computers are. Computers are picky. People are helpful.

Your biggest job as a job seeker is to talk to people. That includes the classic interviewing for a known opening, of course, but it also means talking to *everyone* about your search. It also includes all modalities of contact, face to face, over the phone, via email, even old-fashioned snail mail. It definitely means working your contacts on social sites such as Facebook, LinkedIn, Plaxo, and others.

Once you get to the point where you talk to *strangers* about your job search, you'll be close to getting a job. People in line to buy coffee. Cab drivers. Someone with a cute dog in the park. They're the key. Social scientists have discovered that your first ring of contacts is actually not that useful to you. You have the same knowledge as all your close friends. It's those peripheral people who can connect you to the information that can break open your search.

Most job seekers think you get a job by hiding in the dark, submitting resumes for openings posted on the Internet, and hoping for the best. Wrong, wrong, wrong. You get jobs by talking to people. This has to drive your strategy.

Let me be exceedingly clear: *Talking to computers doesn't count.*

Most jobs are never advertised. More exactly, most people who are hired did not respond to an advertisement of any kind. A job might have been advertised all over the place, but the person who got hired did not apply for that posting. This is critical information for a job seeker who wants to crack the hidden job market.

Think about Internet dating. Wow, are some people liars. They say they're wealthy and sane, when they're broke and crazy. It's the same with hiring. The national lie rate on resumes is about 25 percent. One in four job applicants has an outright lie on the resume. So what do you do about this? You favor candidates who have someone who will vouch for them.

Most people would rather date someone's cousin or coworker than a complete stranger. It's safer. Hiring works the same way. The hiring manager has a stack of 1,000 resumes, and a colleague walks in with a resume and places it on the desk and says, "I know this person. He's sane and presentable." That's a fundamentally different applicant.

Here's a point for you: hiring managers don't need to know you very much. If they know you *at all*, you go to the top of the pile. A friend of an ex-husband's tennis buddy's dog walker's accountant is a close enough connection.

Companies don't make you work too hard to get a job in the hidden job market. For example, they strongly favor hiring candidates who are referred by current employees. One third of companies hire someone for every four people introduced to them by current employees, and another third hire someone for every ten people current employees will vouch for. The last third are more picky, but this is a profoundly important point: in many cases you will need only a handful of personal referrals to land a job! Compare that to the thousands of resumes floating around the Internet, and the thousands of applicants applying for posted openings! (To read about the latest research on the size and nature of the hidden job market, see my website, www.donaldasher.com/hiddenjobmarket.

You may have to move to keep your career on track. Get over it. No place is so special it's worth being homeless there!

The economy is not a smooth batter. It's more like a big cauldron of porridge that's not sitting on the center of the fire. Some places are hot; some places are cool; some are rising; others are in decline. And places that are hot today may be cooling off tomorrow. A welder in Michigan may be barely able to eke out a living, while welders in Wyoming or Louisiana are getting rich. Same skills, different place. An accountant in Cleveland may be treading water, while accountants in Houston have their pick of jobs. Tomorrow it may reverse.

Look around you. Do you see the future or the past? And don't whine to me about your house. If you're upside down on it, give it back to the bank. You'll be a lot better off working in a career-enhancing role in a new locale. If you can't sell it, fill it up with relatives or rent it out. Don't hang on to a declining area until you're flat, busted broke.

If you're a young person without many possessions, couch surfing is a great way to look for work in a distant city. Go to where the opportunity is, if it isn't near you.

Roberto Goizueta, former CEO of Coca-Cola, has this to say about ripples in the economy: "Bad things happen because of what we did in good times. Good things happen because of what we did in bad times." Do something good and move away from bad times if that's what it takes.

Big opportunity is in smaller organizations. Big companies are net destroyers of jobs. Big companies grow through acquisitions. Integrating acquisitions involves firing redundant workers and consolidating processes. Of course, you should look for jobs in big companies, but overlooking the rest of the market is a huge mistake.

The middle market creates permanent jobs. These are companies with $10 to $50 million in annual sales, one hundred to a few thousand employees. Under-the-radar, mid-size companies are the source for most job growth in this country. If you want to read the economic arguments supporting this fact, read the classic *Job Creation in America* (Free Press, 1987) or the more recent *The Great American Jobs Scam* (Berrett-Koehler, 2005).

Small businesses and family businesses with $1 million to $10 million in sales and under 100 employees churn a lot of jobs. They exist in a web of microeconomies. They staff up when they have a run of success, and they staff down when times are tough for them. But for any individual small business *this sequence is often out of sync with the overall economy.* So when times are bad in your industry or in your area, small and family businesses are great sources of continuing career opportunity.

For long-term career management, you may have to change employers more often than you would in a large organization that can provide a smorgasbord of continuing opportunities, but there is opportunity for real success in small and family businesses.

One more advantage to small and family businesses is that they often have trouble attracting talent, which means they're not as picky as Fortune 1000 employers. So if you aren't a perfect candidate for the type of job you want, you definitely need to look at smaller organizations for your next opportunity.

Very small businesses, brand-new startups, and microbusinesses with under a $1 million in annual sales and maybe a handful of employees can be exciting but volatile. You may find yourself promoted to marketing manager at the age of twenty-three, but you may also have to sweep up your own office and carry out your own trash. You can earn major bucks, but you may have to work on commission. And you may go to work one day and find the company shuttered, but these days that could happen even if you work for a hundred-year-old company, like Lehman Brothers.

Contingent jobs are great jobs. Contingent jobs are part-time, temporary, or contract assignments. Many job seekers shun these jobs (until they get desperate). Depending on which source you cite, though, somewhere around 10 percent of all jobs in the economy are contingent. That's a lot of jobs! And here's the clincher: about two-thirds of *new* jobs are contingent when they are created. When a contingent job becomes a permanent one, the incumbent is almost always offered the chance to become a permanent employee in the same role. The trend toward internships and job "tryouts" even for mid-career adults is in full swing. "I've had people who are horrible at interviewing but are awesome employees, and people who are great at interviews and horrible employees," says Steve Newcomb, CEO of Virgance, which partially explains this trend.

This used to be a bottom-feeder area of the economy, but not anymore. There are agencies to help you find contingent jobs all the way up to CEO.

Looking for work is a full-time job. This one you've heard before. You need to treat your job search just as you would your job. There are 168 hours in a week. You need to give up forty of them to find a job. After decades of working with job seekers, I think the best pattern is this: eight hours a day, Monday through Thursday, and you can knock off by noon on Friday. Then on Sunday afternoon, you pick up the project again and plan your week. Nobody works on Friday afternoon anyway, and it's a bad time to contact people.

Monday through Thursday:	8 A.M. to 5 P.M.
Friday:	8 A.M. to noon
Sunday:	1 P.M. to 5 P.M.

You can have the worst strategy in the world, but if you follow this pattern, you'll find a job soon enough. The shocking fact is that most people who are looking for work act like they're on a permanent vacation. My own surveys reveal that the average time a job seeker spends looking for work is six hours a week! And these are people who claim they're actively looking for work "fulltime"!

Interestingly enough, the State of California surveyed this exact same question, and came up with twelve hours per week. It took me some time to realize that people aren't going to tell the State of California that they did nothing last week, zip, zero, nada. Why? Because that would put their unemployment at risk. My surveys turn up a lot of zero hours per week.

One more thing about dedicating forty hours per week to your search: it forces you to find things to do. It forces you to try new avenues, do more and better research, follow up promptly, and be creative to fill the time. Here's the best thing for you to do with your forty hours: identify companies you're interested in, and try to get introduced to people who work at those companies. Remember, a personal referral from a current employee is the number one way companies hire. People you know can lead you to companies you haven't thought of, and they can lead you to people you haven't yet met who can help you find more people and more companies. The key to success is to **talk to people at the companies where you**

want to work. Spend your forty hours a week trying to advance in this activity chart:

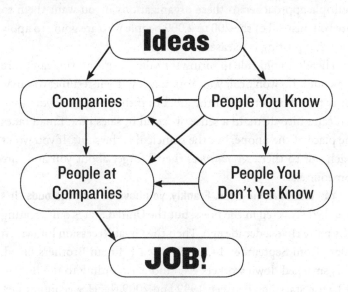

You have to bug people to get hired. You have to make contact several times with an organization to be hired. This will be driven partially by them and partially by you. They'll have a plan to interview you a certain number of times, for example. But you need to have a plan to get into their minds all the while you are under consideration. *Don't ever let a hiring authority forget about you.*

Onetime applications almost never work. If you make contact with a company and they say, "We're not hiring. You're not right for us anyway. We'd never hire you. We don't even like you," then let it go. Move on to the next idea. But if they say, "We're not hiring right now," or "You're not right for the opening we have now," then you've got to design a way to make contact with them over time. We'll look at some cool, creative, and game-changing methods to make contact and stay in contact. Hiring can take weeks, sometimes months, and you need to stay on the radar for the whole time. Never self-select out by fading away.

Most of this book is about how to identify organizations that can hire you *before* they post an opening. But you will have to make multiple approaches to these organizations if you want them to hire you, instead of the 200 to 2,000 people who are going to apply once that posting is released.

There's an old rule in hiring for sales positions: you can't hire someone who won't call you. You may love their resume; you may think they'd be perfect for the job, but if they won't call you, then you can't hire them. In a sense, we're all in sales now. Email takes the place of the phone, but the principal is the same. If you won't reach out to them *several times* they'll forget about you and hire someone else.

You can beat the odds. Frankly, you have to beat the odds. It's been little covered in the press, but the United States quit creating jobs more than a decade ago. Then the Great Recession hit, which I date from September 14, 2008, when Lehman Brothers failed. This smacked down workers even more. According to the Bureau of Labor Statistics, between 1999 and 2009 the U.S. economy created only 121,000 new jobs, a growth rate of .01 percent/year. A decade to create 121,000 net new jobs! It takes 125,000 new jobs *per month* to keep up with population growth alone. It will take considerable time to create enough jobs to absorb the 30 million people who are unemployed, underemployed, or discouraged and off the market as of the day this book went to press.

With this book in your hands, a little strategy, a lot of work, and a little luck, you can find an exciting new job. You can do this even as others around you continue to fail. In short, you can beat them. The goal of this book is to make you faster, better, smarter.

Remember, the overwhelming majority of your fellow citizens are employed. You just want to stay in—or get back into—that part of the population. Even if the economy is tanking precipitously, some people are doing extraordinarily well. Your goal is to be one of the outliers. One of the people who thrives.

No matter what's going on with others, you can beat the odds in the market. Somebody has to, and it may as well be you. Of course, you can beat the odds when things are going well for your industry or area of the country, as well. By mastering the hidden job market you can beat the odds in good times and in bad.

2

HOW THE JOB MARKET REALLY WORKS

A More Sophisticated Definition of the "Hidden Job Market"

To understand the hidden job market you have to understand the total job market, and how organizations fill positions. You have to stop thinking like a job seeker, and start seeing the bigger picture. You are not really important in that bigger picture. Organizations are. So let's think about organizations, and what their needs are.

The hidden job market includes all the jobs that are filled *before* the organization needs to post a recruiting advertisement. No organization needs to go through the hassle of posting an opening and wading through hundreds or thousands of applications if the job is already filled! So those job openings never appear anywhere.

When a worker decides to go back to school or stay home with a new baby, she may do her boss a favor and refer a friend for her position. The boss has a problem, a pending opening. If the boss meets the friend, and decides he can do the job, she may decide that's good enough. Why post the opening and delay the hiring process by four to eight weeks? The friend can have the job. So that job transition never appears anywhere.

And the hidden job market is not just friends hiring friends. **You don't need to have any friends at all to win in the hidden job market.** Companies get applications all the time, in person and online. When a manager needs an employee, she often doesn't have to post an opening. She can just talk to the latest applicant. If the dishwasher or the vice president of sales quits, the manager can just talk to the next dishwasher or sales professional to walk in the door. If that walk-up candidate looks promising enough, the manager can make a hire and get those dishes cleaned or those sales made without going through an expensive and time-consuming recruiting cycle. Those openings will never appear anywhere.

The hidden job market also includes all the jobs that are filled by temporary or contract workers who are asked to join the organization on a permanent, full-time basis. The graphic artist who was doing project work proves so valuable that the boss just decides to bring her on staff. Part-time, temporary, and contract workers are known as contingent workers. Organizations love to convert contingent workers, because they know what they're getting. When contingent workers are converted to permanent employees, their permanent jobs will never have appeared anywhere.

Companies worry about meeting staffing needs, having the right people in the right jobs. So they hold thousands of resumes in their databanks. When they need employees, they don't need to post an opening. They can sort through those thousands of potential employees any time they like. When they hire someone from their databanks to fill an open position, that job opening will not be posted anywhere. It is *hidden* from the general public, and from you.

If you really look at it from the employers' point of view, the only jobs they will need to post are difficult-to-fill positions and bad jobs. If there is a shortage of aerosol engineers, organizations are probably going to have to post some job advertisements to find some. Aerosol engineers who are also fluent in Hungarian, that will definitely be posted everywhere. If a job is horrific or weird, the hiring manager will likely have to advertise to fill it. Cleaning blood from crime scenes? That'll be advertised. Selling water filters to everyone in your social network? That'll be advertised, too. Employers don't need to post openings for easy-to-fill positions, such as marketing assistants, financial analysts, product managers, cost accountants, shipping and receiving clerks, art directors, software developers, and the other jobs that are common in America and Canada today. They keep resume banks full of information on people like that. When they reach into that databank, they are making a placement in the hidden job market. You'll never see that transition from outside the HR office.

Now here's some really big news: *The hidden job market also includes posted openings; it also includes advertised jobs.* They're advertised, all right, but the person who gets hired does not respond to (or perhaps even know about) that advertisement. Why is this? Again, think like an organization. Think like a boss. You have three thousand applicants for a position, and you know that 25 percent of them are lying on their resumes. Your door opens, and one of your employees walks in with a resume. "Hey, I know this guy. I went to school with him. He's okay." What are you going to do? Wade through the three thousand resumes, or talk to the guy your employee knows? That's a big no-brainer.

In short, the hidden job market is any job that you don't see posted. So, it's hidden to you. It may be advertised in forty-foot letters on a sign in Times Square, but you don't know that. The data on the hidden job market prove that people who get jobs are more likely to ignore postings than to pursue them even though lots of those jobs are in fact advertised.

Here are the most important two points for you to know about the hidden job market:

- **At least half of all jobs that change hands go to someone who did not respond to a posted opening.**
- **Only about one-third of open jobs are ever posted anywhere.**

The Overt Job Market

So what's the overt job market? The classic version is the sign in the shop window, "help wanted," and the job postings online or in the newspaper. That's the public job market and, sadly, that's where most job seekers spend all their time. *It's the least productive search methodology, and it sends the job seeker in to the violent maw of horrific competition.* It's the horror film version of the job market. You know there's a job out there somewhere, but you're going to die first because of all the zombies and vampires and alien predators (i.e., your competition) between you and salvation (i.e., the job). It's a video game in which you can't seem to get out of Level One. You keep getting the blue screen of death flashing, "You are out of weapons and energy. You are dead. Goodbye."

Because job postings have mostly migrated from newspapers to online locations, job seekers can now hide in their rooms and "look for a job" twenty-four hours a day. You can imagine them, can't you? Reading instructions, agonizing over the wording of cover emails, copying and pasting resumes, filling out profiles, making sure their attachments have the specified file configuration, registering and inventing user names and passwords, trying to remember if they applied to this position last week, or not. They're communicating with their computer, and their computer is communicating with the employer's computers, *but there's no human on the other end*.

I can actually teach you how to get past resume sorting software, but first I have to drive a stake in this vampire called "posted openings." Job seekers love posted openings for two reasons. First, they believe that there is at least a job behind that posting. At least this company actually has a need for someone like him or her. And second, they like to avoid actually going out in the real world and talking to people. So they love to follow the computerized instructions. It's somehow comforting, no matter how ineffective.

Posted openings are the fool's gold of a job search. They're all bright and shiny, but they are a distraction from your going after the real deal. Have you ever seen kids hunt for Easter eggs? Then you've seen this: a big kid finds an Easter egg, and exclaims her surprise and delight. She hoists that colored egg over her head and shouts in glee, "I found one!" Then all the little kids run over to where she is standing and look near her feet, where there no longer is an Easter egg.

My friend, in the job market you are the little kid. Someone bigger and stronger than you already has that job by the time you apply. Someone with more experience, a higher GPA, a better suit, a more prestigious home address, or a name that reminds the employer of her favorite high school crush. Someone who is not you.

Numbers alone dictate this truth. How many people do you think apply for posted openings? Hundreds and, in some cases, *thousands*. A bar in San Francisco placed an ad on Craigslist for a bartender, and more than 400 people applied! A Catholic church in Minneapolis put an advertisement in the church bulletin for a lunchroom monitor for the local parish school, a minimum wage job, and more than 200 people applied! A trucking company in Indiana put an ad for an administrative assistant on CareerBuilder and between Friday and Monday, 500 people applied! A new store in Tennessee announced job openings, and so many people arrived that there was nearly a riot. It was on the evening news. More than 100 people showed up *in person* for every job posted. The line went around the block. To win a bet, I once ran an ad in the paper, "Hard work, low pay, bad boss. Fax your resume." Seventy-two people applied for this job before I ran out of fax paper! A friend of mine hires PhDs for a biotechnology company. She says she can get at least 200 qualified applicants for any position she posts online. More than 200 people with doctorates!

Can you imagine how many people apply for something like "marketing assistant"? With Monster and CareerBuilder and the other national databases, an employer could choose from *millions* of people who could be a marketing assistant.

One of those millions is going to be the big kid, and you are wasting your time.

There is a curious thing about the psychology of job seekers. They have some mysterious capacity to delude themselves about their chances of winning a posted opening. They say to themselves, "I'm *perfect* for that job. I just know they're going to call me." So they sit at home and wait for that call. They've seen that flashy pyrite, and they think they've struck gold. Here's the unvarnished truth: **job seekers almost always overestimate their own attractiveness, and they underestimate the competition.** No matter how perfect you think you are, there are some really high-quality candidates out there and, to be blunt, a lot of them are more perfect than you.

The job application numbers create brutal scenarios. Resume-sorting software is imperfect; it misses qualified candidates and advances people with the wrong backgrounds. Hiring managers are telling me that rather than sort through hundreds of resumes, they are delighted to consider someone who is referred by an employee or finds some other way to get their attention. Anything rather than winnow a thousand resumes into an interview pool of three to six.

It's hard to stand out in a pile of thousands of resumes. You need to get out of that pile.

Where Jobs Come From

Let's walk through how a new job is created. First, human resources does not create new jobs (except in human resources, of course). They do try to find the right people for jobs, so they're important, but they are not the *source* of new jobs.

Long before human resources gets involved, a line manager decides that she needs help. Workload is expanding, or a key staff member is leaving, or technology and processes evolve and the existing staff do not have the right skill set to cover the changes in the work. The line manager is feeling some pain.

She will feel this pain for quite a while before deciding to hire someone new. She'll overwork the existing staff. She may try to train some of the dullards on her team in the new skills they need before discovering they're incapable of learning them. Or she may plug the gap with temps and contract workers for a while. She'll be in pain for months, sometimes over a year. She'll want to make sure the increased workload or the changes in the work are *permanent* before she makes any staffing adjustments.

Then, finally, she makes the decision. Yep. Gotta hire someone. The stopgap measures have not been to the advantage of the work unit. They're not getting the work done right. So the decision is made. She *intends* to initiate the hiring process. She's still overworked, though, so it gets put off. A week, two weeks, maybe even much longer. The swamp remains full of snapping alligators, so no formal hiring effort gets started right away.

At this stage, she may ask around the work unit if anyone knows someone who can join the team. She may be responsive to networking queries or cold contacts she might have ignored most other times. She'd definitely talk to friends or acquaintances of existing employees if they have the right skill set. Only if none of these people seems right will she initiate the formal staffing requisition process.

Finally, if she has no other choice, she calls human resources. She needs help and she needs it yesterday. She asks them to help her solve her staffing problem. In a day or a week or so, HR sends someone over to analyze the work to be performed, and that person writes a new job description. If HR doesn't have the right resumes in their database, they'll post the opening. It'll take a few more weeks to collect new applications and review resumes, then there are screening interviews by phone, in-person interviews, callbacks, background and reference checks and, finally, an offer and salary negotiation. If you look at it from the organizational point of view, it is no wonder that most managers would do anything to speed this process.

That's where new jobs come from. Remember, somewhere around half of new jobs are filled before they get all the way to the posting stage. Why post a job and create delay and extra work if you can fill it right away? **If you can insert yourself into this process before the job is posted, you can save everyone a lot of time, money, and work.**

Look how late human resources is to this party. The job is created in the work unit. The need is in the work unit. The manager will be unhappy for months and months, and she'll make the decision to hire, and she'll sit on that decision, and only after all that does HR even know about the desire for a new staff member. **You need to insert yourself into this process at the work-unit level.**

The advantages are massive. Not only do you double your access to the job market by accessing all the jobs that are not advertised, but you also reduce your competition by an overwhelming percentage. Let's look at the competition at each stage in the process.

A posted opening draws hundreds or thousands of applicants. So that's the worst spot, in terms of competition, to get involved in the hiring process. But if you walk up to a line manager after she's decided to hire someone, and before she calls HR, *you would have no competition at all.* You'd be the only candidate.

If you contact her while she's overworked and unhappy, your potential competition is her mind-set. She has not decided to solve this problem yet, but if you can convince her that you are a low-risk, high-performer, she may decide to hire you anyway, perhaps on a contract or temporary basis. Remember, about two-thirds of newly created jobs start out as temp or contract assignments.

Once HR is involved, the competition heats up massively. Even at the stage of writing the job description, you're in trouble. HR people are smart about analyzing work. They'll put requirements into the job description that you don't possess. The line manager might take a risk on you if you're from another industry or don't have the right education or credentials, but the HR person won't. The line manager might even prefer to hire someone with most of the right skills and a great attitude, but the HR manager knows that once the position is posted, she can get plenty of applicants who meet *all* the requirements. Once HR is involved, you are disadvantaged.

You need to get into the equation before the manager calls HR. You see that.

You know what's weird? The interesting thing about this explanation is that intelligent people grasp the point. They get it. They realize that all the competition comes after a job is posted, and the easy way to get hired is to approach people before the posting. *And then they'll go hide in their bedroom and keep applying for posted openings in the middle of the night.* It took me some time to realize why this is so. People don't understand how to insert themselves *before the posting* and *at the work-unit level.* That's the hidden job market, and that's what you're going to learn how to do in this book.

3

WHERE ARE YOU GOING?

Stages of a Job Search

Here are the stages of a job search, in the order that you will perform them. Once your job search gets going you will be doing all of this simultaneously, but if you start from scratch, this is the order that you will experience the process:

THE SEVEN STAGES OF A JOB SEARCH

1. Identify job targets (industry, function, title)
2. Identify raw leads (organizations, people, ideas)
3. Convert raw leads into lists of names of specific people
4. Turn a name into an appointment
5. Sell in the interview
6. Stay alive through the selection process
7. Close the deal

We'll be considering every stage more than once as the book progresses, but first you identify a job target. A job target is an idea of a job, and the minimum definition of a job is **industry, function,** and **title.**

You must choose a target industry to find a job in the hidden **job market.** Here are examples of industries: advertising, county government, commercial real estate, construction, K-12 public education, management consulting, hospitals, big-box retail. Industries are clannish. People believe—rightly or wrongly—that as insiders they have special knowledge and that outsiders couldn't possibly understand the nature and the nuances of their work world. Industries are classic organizational silos. They are difficult to enter from the outside, although you can move around within them once you get inside. Some glamour industries are almost impossible to enter except at the entry level, for example, film, fashion, and television.

You must choose a target function to find a job in the hidden **job market.** Here are examples of functions: accounting, sales, customer service, computer programming, training and development, manufacturing, product management, logistics. A function is what you *do* all day long on the job.

You may notice that some industries and functions share the same name, for example, accounting. Accounting is an industry, and most people employed in that industry will perform the function of accounting, but some people working in the accounting industry will be performing administrative, management, public relations, and janitorial functions.

You must discover the title of the job you want in the hidden job market. The title of a job is just its name. Its true definition is the intersection of a vertical line (industry silo) and a horizontal line (function performed). The title is just the name for that intersection. Titles really matter. If you don't know the correct titles for an industry, you're an outsider. And if you're an outsider, you can't be hired. Because you couldn't possibly know the nature and nuances of the insiders' work world *if you don't even know the correct title for a job.*

For example, an editorial assistant and an assistant editor sound kind of the same, don't they? But in publishing, they couldn't be farther apart. An editorial assistant is the lowest human life form in publishing. They make copies and get coffee. The only thing lower than an editorial assistant is an unpublished author. But an assistant editor is just three levels away from divinity itself. Above an assistant editor are only editor, senior editor, publisher, and God.

So you want to work in the movies? You can't if you don't know the difference between a grip and a best boy. Want to work in a public high school? You can't if you don't know the difference between an assistant principal and a dean of students. Again, knowledge of titles identifies you as an insider.

Are you trying to change industry and function at the same time? If so, be sure to start with changing industries as your primary goal. If you are unusually lucky, you may get to make a leap in both categories but, as stated earlier, it is more difficult to enter an industry (a silo), than to move around once you get inside. To break into a new industry may require one step back to position yourself to move two steps forward.

To crack the hidden job market, you identify a job you want and you go look for that type of job. Using hidden job market (HJM) techniques, you actually become more savvy as you look, and you learn more about your target with every contact. You can start out with a naïve idea, such as, "I'd like to work in the movies," and by the end of your search you know perfectly well that a grip sets up camera and electrical equipment, and a best boy reports to a gaffer.

Look for a Certain Type of Job— Don't Look for Openings

When you look for openings you're always a little off center for the assignment; with hundreds if not thousands of applicants, someone else will always be dead center. The differences can be quite subtle, such as the difference between having the experience to be a charge nurse and having the experience to be a nurse supervisor. Let's illustrate the point using the case of a typical college graduate, where the larger mismatch is easy to see.

College graduates who look for work by looking for openings can appear a bit spastic. It doesn't matter whether they majored in art or business. They hear about an opening in commercial real estate, and they run over and beg, "I'd be perfect for this job. I've been in a lot of buildings!" Then they hear about an opening in training and development, and they run over and beg, "I'd be perfect for this position. I've been in the classroom for years!" Then they hear about an opening in retail sales, "I'd be perfect for this position. I love to shop!" I'm not really picking on college graduates, actually. *We all do this.*

When people respond to openings, they can look downright ridiculous. I once had a job candidate who wanted me to help her apply for a posted job in television spot advertising sales, *and her rationale was that she liked to watch TV and knew the shows*. That's bound to win her that job against people with experience in broadcast media advertising sales, right?

Okay, so how do you do it? You pick a **type of job** you want, and you go after it until you are sure that it's not for you, or you land a position. That's it. In a job search, either you decide the direction is not fruitful, or you land a job. Those are the only two outcomes you can allow to happen.

You can't go off in all directions at once. If you want the HJM to work for you, you have to concentrate on a very small list of possible jobs. You can only look effectively for two or three different types of jobs. More than that, and you're just like the college student above. Spastic.

So you run an idea down until you kill it, or it results in a job. Here's an example of running an idea down until you kill it: I had a mid-career client with a background in financial analysis and financial services. He wanted to break into the private equity business. He used HJM techniques to get a series of interviews with private equity professionals, who all told him the same thing: he was too old and expensive to enter the field as an analyst, and not famous or rich enough to enter the field as a deal maker. Ergo, it wasn't going to happen. He didn't let go of his goal when the first person discouraged him. He let it go when he heard identical advice from everyone he was talking with.

Here's an example of running an idea down until you kill it: I had a client who wanted to leave the corporate rat race and work with animals. She volunteered at some veterinary offices, at the ASPCA, and at some animal rescue organizations. She discovered that there was no career position available paying much above minimum wage unless she wanted to go to school for many years to become a veterinarian or scientist. She abandoned her idea of making a paying career of working with animals, but she did continue to volunteer. She didn't back down when the first person told her there was no way for her to make a living at this. She backed down when she found the same story everywhere she looked.

So you have one, two or, at most, three job ideas going. You can only add a new idea when you are sure that one of the ones you are pursuing is a dead end for you.

Here's what the hidden job market looks like when it works correctly.

Aiden Goes Job Hunting

I used to have open office hours on Fridays in the financial district in San Francisco. My office staff gave me all the most interesting clients, basically the ones the other staff thought were crazy or impossible. I actually liked those clients the best.

We were an expensive service, so we didn't get a lot of entry-level candidates. But one Friday, Aiden Spencer comes in and tells me he's a biology major from Cal-Berkeley, about to graduate, and wants our help. He handed me a beautiful resume, already perfect. It described his areas of research experience, and had a lot of bench lab skills and terminology I didn't understand, but it was impressive from top to bottom.

"This looks very good," I said, "but what's spectrophotometry, recombinant DNA technology, and chromatography titration, anyway?" He started to explain, then interrupted himself.

"But I don't want to work in science," he said. "I want to be a residential income property manager."

I looked at him and blurted out the first thing that popped into my mind: "What's that?"

"An apartment manager."

"That's a career job?" I asked, probably failing to hide my concern.

"Sure it is, in a major city," he said. He walked over to my office windows and pointed out buildings from the San Francisco skyline. "That's a residential high-rise, and that's a residential building, and that's a housing co-op. They all have full-time professional staff."

"Okay," I said, "but your resume is all wrong."

"What should I do?" he asked. And in that moment I decided to help this guy find a job for free, just as an experiment.

"Go into those buildings, ask to see the managers, and show them this resume. Ask them, 'What would you need to see on this resume to be interested in hiring me to be an assistant manager in a residential complex like this?' Then follow their advice."

"You can just walk into businesses and ask for a job?" he asked, incredulous.

"Sure," I said, "and sometimes that's the best thing for you to do, if you have no relevant skills at all." We set up a schedule for him to come in every Friday and relay his progress.

The next Friday he came in and reported, "I did what you said. I went in to see a manager, and I showed her my resume, and she looked at it for a while and then said, 'We don't do a lot of biology around here. As a matter of fact, we try to keep biology to a minimum. Why didn't you at least take a few business classes? You'd need to know accounting to work here.' So I told her that I was a treasurer for my fraternity. We bought $23,000 a year in beer alone. I did capital and operating budget projections and variance analyses. It was really like being in charge of a small business."

I looked at his resume, and he had pushed "autoclaves" down a bit, and featured his role as an unpaid treasurer for his fraternity. He had the line about the beer in his description. "Let me give you a tip," I said. "Don't use the word 'beer' anywhere on a college resume, okay?"

The next week he came in and was really excited. "People are starting to talk to me differently," he said. "The first week, it was a glance at my resume and they threw me out in seconds. Now, we're chatting like best friends."

"What's new on your resume?" I inquired.

"This guy asked me if I knew anything about the trades," he said, "and I couldn't understand what he meant. When he told me what the trades were, I realized that I contracted for house repairs all the time. You know a frat house gets some damage on a regular basis, and of course we did upgrades and improvements over the summer." Here was his new listing: "Knowledge of the trades: **Carpentry, Plumbing, Electrical, Painting,** including putting projects to bid, selecting contractors, and supervising workers on site."

"Protein synthesis" was now even further down on his resume, and the whole top of the page featured aspects of his work with the fraternity and their house. I also noticed he had changed the word "beer" to "liquid refreshments."

The next week he came in truly excited. "I went in to see this guy, and he really warmed up to me. 'I'd love to hire you,' he said, 'but our whole crew speaks Spanish, so you have to speak Spanish to work here.' And I was able to say to him, '*Pero yo hablo un poco español!*'"

"Where'd you learn Spanish?" I interrupted.

"Spring break," Aiden said. "I did the whole Rosetta Stone thing. It's not that hard if you work at it. He didn't hire me after all, but this was a really important thing to find out."

There was no longer any room on his resume for "endonucleases," whatever they are. He was learning the lingo that residential income property managers use, and his resume had the right information on it. Then he really disappointed me the next week.

"I made a major decision," he said. "I don't want to be an apartment manager after all."

I was stunned. "But you just spent four weeks on this. You're about to get a job, I just know it."

"No. I made a shift. I want to be a commercial property manager."

"But that's a credentialed position in California," I explained. "You don't have the credential. You can't get that."

"No, you're wrong," he protested. "The senior manager on property usually has a credential, and it's not even a legal requirement. All the assistant managers and leasing agents work under the senior manager's authority. See, I know something you don't. You should get out more."

So this shift in focus actually capitalized on his prior work. I sent him out into the financial district of San Francisco confident that he would get a job soon, and he did. It took another two weeks, and then he came in gushing.

"I got a job! I'm a leasing agent, and I'm in charge of the tenant newsletter! You're not going to believe how fast I was able to use what I learned this week. I was in 450 Market, trying to get this guy to hire me. He said he had an opening for a leasing agent, but he didn't like me. He said, 'You don't even know what a triple-net lease is.' So I said, 'What's a triple-net lease? Can you show me one?' He says, 'It's monthly rent, plus pass through for utilities, plus a periodic or annual assessment for maintenance. And no, you can't look at one of our lease agreements.' So I walked across the street to 455 Market, walked in to the management office, and said I wanted to apply for a job as a leasing agent. 'I know what a triple-net lease is. I know how to talk about tenant improvements and even how to do a back-of-the-envelope estimate of TI costs, based on my knowledge of the trades and my prior experience supervising contractors and subs, so I can do this job. And I speak Spanish. I even have my own laser tape,' and I showed her this laser I got from Home Depot that measures down to the 1/8 of an inch. You can also set it to do metric. We started talking about my tape, and about contractors, and utility trunks, and before I knew it, I was hired on the spot. I start tomorrow morning at 8 A.M."

My biologist did a perfect job of finding a job in the hidden job market. He went looking for a certain type of job. He never once worried about looking for an opening. He got people to talk to him. He used what he learned from these conversations to be a better candidate. He improved his resume and incorporated skills he gained outside of regular employment. He did let his goal evolve, but in a way that actually worked better for him. That's the formula for career success. It's simple. It's effective. And it works awesomely whether you're a high school dropout or a six-figure executive.

THE FORMULA FOR CAREER SUCCESS

1. Identify a job target of interest.
2. Find someone doing that job *right now*.
3. Talk to him/her.
4. Repeat until hired.

What You Seek Is What You Will Find

Make a list now of one to five targets that are desirable to you. Put in obvious jobs, like ones you have done recently or in the past, but also throw in some dream jobs or some jobs you believe you have the skills to do but have not yet been employed to do.

The most obvious targets for you to seek are jobs that are highly related to the job you have now (or the last job you held). You're already in the industry, you already know the lingo and the secret handshake.

Your latest employer's competitors are the most obvious places for you to seek your next assignment. If you worked most recently in public accounting or big-box retail, then the obvious place to start your job search is with *other* public accounting firms and *other* big-box retail stores.

Before you give up on your current or former employer, ask yourself if there is a possible home for you somewhere else in the organization. Is there a branch or an affiliate that you would be happier working for? Is there a function, other than the one you're doing now, that would reexcite you and reenergize your career? If so, put that on your target list.

Your former employer's customers or clients are also obvious places for you to consider. You know some things about their world that outsiders wouldn't know. It's the same with vendors or suppliers to your old employer. Finally, any venture partners or consultants to your former employer are places where you have special knowledge that may help you get into their silos.

Or you could go in a new direction entirely. One of the coolest parts of the HJM system is that it allows you to pursue dream jobs even if you've never done anything about that dream before. If you've always wanted to be an alternative-rock star, or a nightclub bouncer, or a museum docent, or an international sales rep, or a mattress tester, you can put that on your list.

Remember to think about whether this career idea will lead to your being able to pay your rent or mortgage, eat well, and so on. Adults support themselves and their families, so that has to be part of your plan. Otherwise, that idea might make a better target for a hobby than a job.

Be very specific. Your targets need to be fully formed ideas. "Something on Wall Street" is not at all a career target. "Buy-side equity analyst" is. You will find when you go out to approach people that nobody wants to help someone who says, "I'm interested in doing *anything* in your industry." That's certainly a sincere desire, *but how do you help a person like that?* You can't. That's like holding a map and asking strangers on a street corner, "I'm looking for a place, but I don't know where it is."

"What place?" someone overly helpful might attempt.

"I don't know, but it's on this map."

You will find that they will edge away from you, and then possibly run.

Remember the biologist Aiden Spencer, a few pages back? He got so far so fast because he started with a specific goal: residential income property management in San Francisco. That guided his actions. He knew what he was looking for on the map.

Specificity supports action. The more specific you are, the more people can tell you how to achieve or approach your goal. This is not actionable: "I'm looking for something to do with the environment, or something in green business."

These are excellent target statements:

"I am looking for something in green building certification in Chicago, or green roof design for high-rise buildings. I have two goals: to discover who is doing green building certification in Illinois, and to discover who is doing work on green roofs. You know, where they basically put a park on top of a building to the benefit of the building, the people in it, and the environment as a whole."

"I'm interested in learning more about industrial-level recycling of post-consumer electronics, as in container loads or larger, and global trade in such materials. I am particularly interested in unit- and component-level reuse applications, where computers and cell phones and TVs and so on are sold whole or in batches of de-manufactured parts to small businesses in the developing world. I don't care where the business is located, as long as it is a global player."

Just for the record, my favorite target of all time came from a college student in a workshop: "I am interested in practical, real-world applications for Chaos Theory. I would like to be a 'Chaos Theory consultant' for government or industry or a think tank, maybe even the CIA."

Pick things that can sustain your interest. If you are fascinated by your work, passionately interested in it, you'll work harder. Your hard work will be noticed. You'll get promoted. You'll be offered more opportunity. You'll be able to enlist other people in your ideas. You'll accrue power and, with it, the chance to do good things. Favor job targets that excite you.

Write your job targets now, one to five. Write as much as you can imagine of the jobs you want to seek: industry, function, title, compensation, location, level of authority, type of organization, position in the market, size, how often you will travel, and even what you think you'll wear to work. Be very specific, because that will help you get started.

Then, pick the three or fewer that you will focus on to start your job search. You can't effectively look in more than three directions at the same time. You can add one new idea every time you run an existing target down and kill it.

JUST FOR FUN—CALL THEM UP!

I don't want you to be bored so early in this book, so I'll share with you the fastest way to get a job in the whole world: pick up the phone and call businesses. Email also works, but not as well. Simply call or email smaller companies and ask them if they're considering hiring someone like you. This doesn't work with large companies because there are so many layers between the front door and an actual hiring manager. But with smaller companies it works great. If you want to work at a pizza shop or a CPA firm or a company that tutors K-12 students in math or reading, all you have to do is build a list of them and start calling. "I wonder if you're thinking about hiring a marketing assistant. Who would I talk to about that?" Then, follow the instructions of the person who answers the phone. Email is okay, but phone calls have a much higher response rate; it's too easy to ignore an email.

I often give this advice in workshops, as a joke, of course: you can call anyone up and say, "I heard you were looking for a cost accountant. Who would I talk to about that?" Now, I think it is very important to always tell the truth in all situations. So right before you make the call to XYZ Corp, say out loud, "XYZ Corp is looking for a cost accountant." When you speak, you also hear, so you can then immediately and truthfully say, "I heard you were looking for a cost accountant." If they press you for where you got this information, you can truthfully say, "I overheard it in my neighborhood."

All joking aside, you can call anyone up and ask, "I wonder if you're thinking about hiring a _____. Who would I talk to about that?"

If you want to be vice president of finance, you might want to dress up your approach a bit by mentioning a mutual acquaintance or providing information about how you got the person's name, but the basic technique remains the same.

Do You Have A Career Emergency?

Most career emergencies are resume problems. For example, there are resume techniques to disguise long-term unemployment. There are ways to look for work long-distance and even look like a local from anywhere in the country. There are resume techniques that allow you to slant your skills toward a new industry. There are solutions to that old conundrum that bedevils career changers and college students: you have to have experience to get a job, and you have to have a job to get experience. For example, if you fear employers will think you're too old, there is a quick and easy resume solution. Just list the last ten years or so of experience, and omit the dates from your education. Voilà! You are timeless.

For resume solutions to career problems, see my companion book, *The Overnight Resume*. Solutions to all common career problems are in that guide.

Don't worry: emergencies have solutions. If you are nearly out of money, you have a career emergency. You need a job ASAP, and you can't afford to be too picky. If you're in an area of the country with very high and endemic unemployment you may need to move to another part of the country to find success. If you're in a field that is moribund, you may need to apply your transferrable skills in a new profession. That's hard to do, and needing to find a new profession can become a career emergency, too. If you're a parent returning to the workforce or just released from a long stint as a prisoner, you have a career emergency. Interestingly, prisoners and stay-at-home moms and dads have the same exact career problem.

Effort will solve many career problems. If you have a bad resume and a bad suit, but you walk into businesses from 8 A.M. to 5 P.M. every day with a smile and ask for the manager, you'll get a job soon enough. In fact, you could stand at the end of an off ramp wearing a sign "Professional Out of Work, 3 Kids, Savings Gone, Please Stop and Take a Resume." If you did it all day every day, you'd get a job sooner than later. (I have a file of newspaper clippings about job seekers who did some version of this and all of them were successful, some after the local news covered their unusual exertions.)

No amount of effort is going to get a job to come open that simply isn't there, however. If you want to be an international fashion model, you can't stay in Peoria. If you want to be a $250,000 executive, and there are no $250,000 jobs near the small-town university where your spouse is earning a PhD, then I see compromise coming up in your future.

One solution to many career problems is to *keep looking while you have a job.* Don't be satisfied with that imperfect job and continue to look, look, look until you get an appointment that meets all or most of your goals for job, salary, and location. Yes, if you do this you will hop through some assignments along the way, but tenure at bad jobs is vastly overrated. Why stay in a bad job so you can show on your resume that you stayed in a bad job longer?

Job hopping, especially for people facing career emergencies, is often the smartest thing a person can do. Get a job, get some income, prove and improve your skills, and constantly seek a better job to climb up the ladder. For young people just trying to establish themselves, for prisoners just released from incarceration, for stay-at-home moms and dads trying to reenter the professional world, for people dealing with long-term unemployment, and for people new to a town or region, this is often the best career strategy to advance into higher pay and greater responsibility.

This is called "bouncing." Think of a pogo stick. You're bouncing through interim jobs to get back to a significant level of responsibility and income.

The reason that no one advocates for this (besides me) is that it doesn't serve organizations' needs. It's not best for organizations, which don't like to train people and lose them. But it can be a fantastic strategy for highly talented workers who find themselves in career emergencies.

Do you need to make some adjustments in your plans? **Magical thinking doesn't work.**

What's Your Best Option?

Now, considering the above ways to address career emergencies, is there any adjustment to your target? What one, two, or three *specific* jobs are you interested in seeking? Write these out now, because moving forward in the book it is assumed that you have identified one (or a few) particular jobs of interest.

4

HOW to MEASURE YOUR SEARCH ACTIVITIES

The Three Truths of a Job Search

There are only three things you need to know about job change:

1. You get jobs by talking to people.
2. You look for work in channels.
3. You need 100 leads at all times.

You get jobs by talking to people. I cannot emphasize this enough. Anything that you do that causes you to talk to *people* speeds your job search, and anything you do that keeps you from talking to *people* slows down your job search. I have suggestions for shy people coming up, so no one gets a pass on this. Emails and phone calls do count as "talking to people."

Acknowledgment Notices and Ding Letters

When your computer talks to a company's recruiting website, it will often generate a nice little email that may lead you to believe that a human being has looked at your resume. "Thank you for your recent application to Really Good Corporation. We appreciate your interest in employment with us. We are diligently comparing your qualifications and experience to our staffing needs, and will be in touch with you shortly if we see a match. Your information will be automatically kept on file for six months so there is no need to contact us again."

As an experiment, I submitted fake resumes for a guard dog named "Rex" to several corporate websites. "Rex K. Nine" clearly was a dog. He was looking for "kibbles" for pay. Rex's skills included "guarding warehouses and junkyards" and "able to bite unauthorized personnel in buttocks if they fail to show appropriate identification." Rex got a nice set of responses exactly like the above. *Acknowledgment emails mean nothing.*

When you apply for a specific opening, some employers are kind enough to send you ding letters that let you know that you are no longer under consideration. Either they have hired someone else, or they have actually—for real—looked at your background and they don't see a match. This closes that application for you. This is a gift, because for all open items (your applications that haven't received a negative response, yet), you need to keep tickling them from time to time until they say that they've hired someone else or they don't like you for the position. So ding letters are actually a good thing for you. They help you manage your search process.

If you don't get a ding letter, assume you're still under consideration. Employers stop and start recruitment efforts all the time. They may put a freeze on a hiring project, or they go a full round of interviews and don't find anyone they like, or a key boss is out of town or on a special assignment and the recruitment effort stalls, or they hire someone and he fails to show up for the first day of work as expected. So don't assume you're not in the game unless they tell you so. A staffing requisition can run four months, or more, from the time human resources posts an opening and a new employee starts the job. There's more on how to manage the candidate-employer relationship over this long, drawn-out process in chapter 13: Staying Alive, beginning on page 181.

I got a wonderful twist on a ding letter off the Internet, original author unknown, and published it in a prior book. During the trials and tribulations of your job search, you might enjoy reading this from time to time:

Dear Mr. Steel:

Thank you for your kind letter of April 17. After careful consideration I regret to inform you that I am unable to accept your refusal to offer me employment with your firm.

This year I have been particularly fortunate in receiving an unusually large number of rejection letters. With such a varied and promising field of candidates, it is impossible for me to accept all refusals.

Despite your outstanding qualifications and previous experience in rejecting applicants, I find that your rejection does not meet my needs at this time. Therefore, I will initiate employment with your firm immediately following graduation. I look forward to seeing you then.

Best of luck in rejecting future candidates.

Sincerely,
Anthony T. Tyger

I was driving on the Pennsylvania turnpike one day, and heard on NPR a student describing how he had used this letter *and it had worked!* The company called and said, "You're pretty funny. We're going to take another look at you." He was eventually hired. My advice: enjoy this as a joke, but don't use it. Too many people have seen it. There are now more than 240,000 listings on the Internet featuring this letter, so you're too late for this one.

You look for work in channels. You look for a certain type of job, rather than for posted openings. We covered this in the last chapter. You can run a great job search by ignoring posted openings altogether, but in any case *the bulk of your search efforts will be to seek a certain type of job whether or not any specific organization has a posted opening in that area.* That's what it means to look for work in channels, rather than jumping around trying to repackage and reposition yourself to fit one posted opening after another. You're not going to be perfect, and some big kid is going to get those jobs.

You need 100 leads at all times. You will need to do *research* to do a *job search*. Don't worry about how to do research. I will teach you quick and easy ways to find companies that match your interests. But you must accept the basic fact: research is required. You probably do not know, right now, the company that's going to hire you.

You also need 100 leads to drive your activity. You need 100 leads so you can abuse a lead, annoy her, or break a few rules. Who cares if someone gets mad at you, if you have ninety-nine more leads behind that one? Who cares if you call someone one time too often, or email him until he writes back to you with a flaming "unsubscribe"? When a lead dies, you just replace it with a new lead, to always have at least 100. Having 100 leads creates discipline, and keeps you busy. It frees you up to be a more aggressive—and ultimately more successful—job seeker.

Besides, there is one more secret to having 100 leads. We know from research done by members of the Direct Marketing Association, those wonderful people who bring you spam, junk mail, and telephone solicitations, that if you approach 100 people about almost anything, you can get a positive response rate of between .05 and 4 percent. A job search is an interesting form of sales campaign. You need only one "yes" to get you back into the happily employed category. So, having 100 leads creates a high likelihood that somewhere in that pile is the one "yes" you need.

Measure What Matters

My brother, a really smart guy, told me that he was looking for work and he was following all my advice. "Great," I said. "How many face-to-face meetings did you have last week, and how many applications do you have active right now?"

"Face-to-face meetings?" he asked. "Active applications?"

"Yeah," I said. "How many people did you look in the eye and shake hands with this week, and how many recent applications do you have where you've applied and they have not yet dinged you?"

"Well, I didn't meet anyone this week," he admitted. "No one's called me for an interview yet. And I applied for eight jobs so far, I think."

"Then you're profoundly not following my advice," I said. "What did you do on the afternoon of the first day of your job search? You could apply for eight jobs in about an hour and a half. You need to restructure your whole approach, or you're going to go broke, you'll lose your house, your new Porsche will be repossessed, your wife will leave you, your kid will call someone else 'Daddy,' and you'll end up living on my couch. I can't allow that last thing to happen, so let's replan this whole process." Well, I didn't say it *exactly* that way, but that's pretty close. And he did have a new Porsche, and not a nickel of savings. And I don't care how much he protests; I did catch him glancing a little too fondly at my couch.

How do you know you're doing a good job in your job search? *Raw activity is not enough.* You can be really busy in a job search while nothing is really happening. If your computer talks to some corporation's computer, that's nothing. That counts for nothing.

The most important thing to measure is actual interviews for jobs. Everything else is secondary. **If you get interviews, you'll get a job. If you don't, you won't.** It's that simple.

I once watched a guy who didn't speak a word of English get a job in half an hour. He was walking down Polk Street in San Francisco. He went into each shop and restaurant and approached the best-dressed person in each. He'd stick out his hand and say, "Excuse me, mister. Do you have a job?" He even picked out people on the sidewalk. "Excuse me, mister. Do you have a job?" How do I know he didn't speak English? He used the same words with women, "Excuse me, mister. Do you have a job?"

He got a job in half an hour, while with all your privileges it may take you months. But his technique had one wonderful effect: he was getting an interview every few minutes! You need to follow his example and get out there and stick out your hand and ask people, "Excuse me, mister. Do you have a job?"

You need face time to get a job. Interviewing for possible jobs is the most important activity in a job search, but any kind of face time will lead you to your goal, even if you don't speak English or you have a greasy mullet from 1989.

Remember, you're going to look for work forty hours a week, all day Monday through Thursday, a half day on Friday, and a half day on Sunday. Every Sunday you should evaluate the prior week's efforts, and plan the coming week's activities. Here's what to measure:

New people you've met face to face. That's the number of new people each week you look in the eyeball and ask for help in your search. Three is a minimum. You have to get out of the house. Keep meetings to coffee, so you don't have to buy anyone's lunch or dinner. A lot of these meetings will amount to nothing, but it keeps your conversational skills sharp. You'll stay fluent in presenting what you're looking for and what skills you have to offer.

New people you've met online. Five is a minimum. If you can't meet five new people online in a week, you're not trying at all. People you know will introduce you to people you don't, and it's easy. "Friending" and "linking" and spamming don't count, but trading emails with a sentient human being does. If you write to someone and she creates a unique, thought-out response just for you, that counts as "meeting someone" online.

New posted openings you've applied for. In spite of the fact that this has a low return on effort, of course you will apply for posted openings that you find that match your interests! Ten brand-new applications per week is a minimum. As I've mentioned, posted openings are actually a great place to get career ideas. If one company is advertising a job you find attractive, find *all the other companies like that one* and approach them all about that type of position.

New organizations you've found that "might" harbor a job you want. Finding ten brand-new companies every single week that might be able to hire you is a minimum. You'll be doing research on an ongoing basis to keep this quantity up. Once you decide on the type of job you're after (previous chapter), you'll be building lists of organizations that hire people to do that type of job (next chapter). Ten might not seem like many, but once a company is on your list, you'll be approaching it over and over and in myriad ways, so the work will snowball over time for each company on your active lists.

Interviews for information. This is a key hidden job market search technique. You'll need two informational interviews a week to run an effective campaign. The technique is described in detail in chapter 10, Engaging Possible Employers, beginning on page 127.

Screening interviews with a real possible employer. A screening interview is a 5- to 10- minute interview by phone or in person to see if you are a viable candidate for a position. A "real possible employer" is someone who has responded to your application for a posted opening, or someone who has agreed to speak with you about employing you with her organization. Screening interviews are hard to count, because sometimes an employer will start screening you and then turn the call or visit into a real interview. Other times calls that start out as networking attempts slip subtly into screening interviews. Finally, you may advance to an extended, face-to-face interview without ever having endured a screening interview. Nevertheless, try to identify and count screening interviews, in part so you can calculate conversion rates (more on that in just a moment).

First interviews for a "possible" job. This includes interviews for posted openings, and interviews with an organization that doesn't have a posted opening but has agreed to meet with you about employing you. *This is the step that counts!* All your other effort is designed to create more first interviews. This is how you get a job! This is the metric that matters! Do you get it, or do I need to use more exclamation points?! Okay, you get it. If you're running a good search, you should be able to get two of these per month, *minimum.* Depending on the field and the level of the job, this will be easy or difficult, but for pretty much everybody, two first interviews per month for a possible job is required to eventually find success.

Conversions. You should convert about half of your screening interviews into an extended job interview. Likewise, you should be able to convert about half of your first interviews into continuing interviews. This is important for you to keep track of. If you have lots of interviews for real possible jobs but you never get any callbacks or offers, you may have an interviewing problem.

Follow-up interviews. Almost no one hires on a first interview, so you may have second and third, all the way up to six interviews to land an offer. Success in staying alive and continuing to get call-backs is a critical part of running a job search, as employers take months to hire, and different people want to meet you. The search requisition itself may evolve, as well, so lots of meetings are a common part of the job market now. Count all your follow-up interviews for a possible job; it will help you keep track of which possible employers you need to give more attention to as time passes.

Active items, aka open items. This is everyone you owe a phone call to, everyone you agreed to "check back in with" by a certain date, every job you've applied to where they have not yet sent you a ding letter, everyone who said, "Why don't you give us a call at the first of the month," everyone who said, "We'll let you know when we're ready to start interviewing," and so on. In any active job search you will and should have dozens of these. Count them, also.

Dings. Those are "possible jobs" for which you are rejected, plus open items that you now realize are dead. You should count your dings just so you can see progress. Every time you get interviewed for a real possible job is a success story in a job search, whether you get a job offer or a ding letter. So count them and celebrate them. Ironically, they prove that you are doing many things right.

Offers. Yes, if you do this right, you'll start to get job offers. Some of them won't be right for you, and you'll decline them. Job offers are sweet, even those you decline, so count them, too. Since most employers look at three finalists for every hire, average applicants should get an offer about one-third of the time they're interviewed for a possible job.

Self-assessment and **goals for the coming week.** Of course you will want to assess whether you have met your objectives for the week past, and you'll want to set goals for job search activity for the coming week.

Finally, you may want to consider if you have any systemic performance problems. Ask yourself, **How am I stopping myself from succeeding** and **how can I overcome that blockage?** Everyone has habits, legacies from his family and upbringing, and parts of her self-image that are counterproductive to performance in a job search. Frankly, no one is immune from this, even highly successful people. It is helpful to name these problems, and identify for yourself ways to combat these negative habits and scripts. Taking a few minutes once a week to identify and plan to combat these issues is well worth the introspection.

All in all, the most important basic metric to track is "new people met face to face." If that number is consistently high, you're going to get a job. Take some time every week to review your prior week's search efforts, and plan the coming week's activities. Do it the same time every week. I suggest Sunday afternoon. Here's what to count in your job search:

SUNDAY NIGHT SCORECARD

Over the past week. . .

New people met face to face: (3 per week minimum)

New people met online: (5 per week minimum)

New posted openings applied for: (10 per week minimum)

New organizations found: (10 per week minimum)

Interviews for information: (2 per week minimum)

Screening interviews for a possible job (phone or in person):
(no specific minimum)

First-time interviews for a possible job: (2 per month minimum)

Conversion ratio of follow-up interviews: (should be more than 50%)

Total number of active items, aka open items: (should be dozens)

Dings: (no specific minimum)

Offers: (accepted, rejected, or pending)

Self-assessment of my performance for the week:

Goals for the coming week:

How am I stopping myself from succeeding?

How can I overcome that blockage?

Tracking Open Items

Even with a modest goal for *new* contacts per week, you'll soon have hundreds of details to manage in your job search. You'll need to keep track of when to call or email people, when to tickle employers about applications that have stalled, when to inquire about second interviews, and so on. **The date of your next contact is the key information item to track.** How to track each job-search step is explained in chapter 6, Managing Hundreds of Leads, beginning on page 77.

5

BUILDING

LEAD LISTS

Becoming Systematic

One of the really big problems for most job seekers is that they are not systematic at all. One day they're looking for some kind of administrative job on Craigslist, and the next day they're down at Macys applying for holiday jobs, then they're calling their former sorority sister to ask if she has any suggestions, and after that they're trying to convince the principal down at their kids' school that they'd be an excellent classroom paraprofessional. They're not systematic in two key areas:

1. Their target, that is, the *kind* of job they're after, and
2. Their methodology, that is, the *way* they look for work.

You will be systematic! It's easy to be systematic in an HJM search because you don't care whether an employer is advertising openings or not. That's completely irrelevant to your search. You have only one or two or three job targets at a time, and you don't flit from idea to idea. You run an idea down and kill it before moving on. That's the system you want to follow.

You need to *systematically* build lead lists, and *systematically* work them. This is Stage Two of your job search: **identifying raw leads.** Job leads are the raw material of your job search. You'll consume them on a daily basis. A job lead is a cousin, a friend of a friend, a promising ad online, or an article in the business section of the newspaper. Now that you have a target in mind, a specific target, you need to start building lead lists.

Although "raw" job leads may be as nebulous as an idea or a comment overheard at a coffee shop, all job leads can be distilled eventually into three categories: organizations, people, and ideas.

For our purposes, **organizations** are defined as potential employers. So you will want to build lists of every employer that is related to your job targets. Not some. *Every single appropriate employer in your target geographical areas.*

And you will want to build lead lists of **people,** of *every* person who could help you in your job search, not just the powerful and well-connected friends and acquaintances. *Every single person who could help you.*

And even **ideas** can be raw leads. An idea might be something like "I wonder if there is any way to make money with my hobby of lewd cake decorating?" or "I've been laid off three times in the past two years. Is there anyone who is a 'layoff consultant'? Maybe they're doing booming business. Wasn't there a movie about that?" or "Those buildings on Sand Hill Road, they all seem to be full of thriving firms. Maybe I could just go over there and write down the names of businesses with the lights on, and then go look up what they do," or "Kids. There are lots of kids in my neighborhood. More than I've ever noticed in the past. Surely somebody is selling something to families with kids," or "Bob? No, I think his name is Bub. Yeah, Bub Williams! That guy always seems to have plenty of loose cash. I wonder what he is doing for a living," or "Hhhhmmn. Johnson Controls just signed a big lease for an industrial building. I wonder if I could get a list of other companies who've signed leases in our town over the past two years. A company signing a big, new lease must be growing." Those are the kind of ruminations that can drive a creative and dynamic job search. You want to write down your ideas as they occur to you, and treat them as high-value job leads.

Ideas are an interesting form of raw lead. If you look carefully at ideas, the ones that work out quickly lead to lists of organizations and people.

Let's review all the good sources of raw leads, then we'll look at converting a raw lead into the name of a specific person to contact or, more often, a *list of specific people* to contact.

WARNING: This is the densest chapter in this book, so if this is not the right time for you to wade through the information here, skim it. It will be waiting for you when you need it, in all its great and glorious detail. Do define your job target, however. See stage one, "Identify job targets," page 24. Your goal is to be working with 100 leads at all times. Any time you do not have 100 leads, revisit this chapter.

Great Sources of Raw Leads

Your existing job targets. Once you have an idea of the type of job you would like, you can build lists of companies that have that type of job. Your job search work is then driven by the idea you have of the job you want to obtain. After reading the previous chapters, you should already have a list of three to five fully formed job ideas. If not, reread chapter 3. Your next step is to build lists of companies or organizations that have those types of jobs.

Job postings. The best way to use job postings is not to apply for those postings you find, but to use the postings to generate ideas of jobs you might like. So if you find a job posting for a recreational director for a senior center, then you would make a list of *all* the senior centers and assisted living facilities in your target geographical areas to see if any of them have the position of recreational director, and to explore service companies like Exploritas (formerly Elderhostel) to see how they plan their programming. See how this works?

Gossip. You're going to be emailing, texting, calling, interviewing, and catching coffee or lunch with a steady stream of people, and they're going to throw ideas at you every day. Some of these ideas are going to be goofy or obscure, but take them all seriously. If you've never thought about working as a counselor for a Christian weight loss program, or serving as a senior advocate, or learning more about the exciting world of a product demonstrator, now's your chance.

The business news. The business news is full of raw leads. Companies that are forming, expanding, or relocating are obviously attractive to job seekers, but also any company doing anything interesting should gain your attention. A management shakeup, a new technology implementation, a new product release, the arrest of a prominent company officer, all of these spell opportunity!

Job fairs. Recruiters go to job fairs to show face, that is, to keep their name out there, and also to fill obscure and hard-to-fill openings. So, they're a good place to get ideas of what employers are looking for today. Remember that they're going to post signs for truly difficult-to-fill assignments, like ADA Compliance Attorney or Plastic Extrusion System Design Engineer, but they're also always hiring for all the usual positions all organizations need. In a down economy, however, job fairs can be frustrating and depressing, so if the market is tight in your area, you might better put your energy elsewhere.

Search engine expeditions. When you're bored and running low on leads, search any idea you can think of, from "corporate ethics" to "sports medicine in Ohio" to "internships with sea turtles." This will provide you with a mix of raw leads (newspaper articles, blogs, websites), both legit and nonlegit. You can then follow up on what you find.

Anytime your job-search ideas are getting stale, revisit these sources of raw leads. Run a search on:

- "can't be outsourced"
- "recession-proof careers"
- "rapidly growing" PLUS name of your town
- "new jobs" PLUS name of your town
- "new lease" PLUS name of your town
- "newly hired" PLUS name of your town
- "was promoted" PLUS name of your town
- "doing really well" PLUS name of your town
- "great new" PLUS name of your town
- "new company" PLUS name of your town
- "economic success" PLUS name of your town
- "consulting" PLUS name of your town

- "economic growth"
- "safe from a downturn"
- "qualified workers" or "qualified employees"
- "job openings"
- "fast-growing company" or "fastest growing company"
- And any similar search terms that you believe will lead you to opportunity.

People Who Want to Help You

You get jobs by talking to people. We covered that point earlier. People are your biggest asset in a job search, and you will approach them systematically and methodically. In the next chapter we'll explore how to do this most effectively, but first we have to build some lead lists.

Think like a big-hearted extrovert, even if you're not naturally like that. Suppose you wanted to have a really big party and you had an unlimited budget to throw this party. Let's imagine that you won a Nobel Prize or you were going to marry a very wealthy, generous, and gregarious spouse. "Good on you," as the Australians say. You'd want to invite everyone you'd ever known or touched, right? Well, that's a great place to start building a lead list for your job search.

People actually know hundreds or thousands of other people. People are hardwired to live in villages with up to 150 friends (*The Tipping Point* by Malcolm Gladwell, Back Bay Books, 2002). An adult American knows at least 600 people, and a British social networking researcher recently found that some people know as many as 10,000 people! A lot of potential contacts on your lists will be kind of vague at first, like "my lab partner from freshman biology" or "my hairdresser's two colleagues" or "everyone on my mailing list for fans of BR-549." It's not necessary to know their names in order to put them down as potential assets.

Some items on your list will be individual people, like the super for your apartment building, and others will be portals to a category of person, like the music mailing list just mentioned, or all the alumni of your college, or all the members of your church, synagogue, mosque, or ashram. Obviously, all your friends on Facebook or connections on LinkedIn are one of the first items to go on these lists. So you see that some items on your lists will actually be megalistings, categories leading to possibly thousands of people with whom you have a preexisting connection.

Avoid the natural tendency to handicap your lists. You may want to concentrate on powerful people, or people in certain industries, but frankly, you need to put down everyone you can think of. The reason is simple. Unusual connections are the norm in a job search.

You can't foretell who can help you. A friend of mine is a mid-level movie producer who at one point was "on the beach" or "between pictures," as they like to say in that business. The fact was, he was unemployed and getting concerned about it. He looked at his dog walker one day and thought, I bet some of her other clients are in the business. "Dee," he asked, "do you know anyone making a film right now, maybe they're out of town a lot."

"Sure," she said, and named someone he knew of, but did not know directly. To make a long story short, his dog walker introduced him to one of her other clients, and he got an assignment as a second-unit director on a feature film.

People with no power often have the information you need.

Here's another one: I had a heckler in a workshop I was giving at a major university. He was a doubter, who was sitting in the front row, and he was infecting my audience. When I got to this part in the presentation, making lists of everyone you know, he piped up, "I don't think this will work. You want to concentrate on people in the field and not waste your time on people who don't know anything about what you're after. I'm interested in biotechnology. My Aunt Ruth in Florida is not going to know anything about biotechnology."

And in that moment, I took one of the biggest risks I've ever taken as a speaker. "Let's call her up," I dared. "Let's see if you're right. Do you know her number?"

He whips out his cell phone, and we ring up Aunt Ruthie. She sounds like she's 110 years old, and he says to her, "Aunt Ruthie, this is Bobbie. I'm in a career workshop, and this guy's making us call up people and ask them for job leads. I'm wondering if you know anyone in the biotechnology field."

There was a long pause, then Aunt Ruthie said, in a slow and shaky voice, "No, Bobbie. I don't know anyone in biotechnology. But I do have some biotechnology stocks in my portfolio. Maybe one of them would be interesting to you. Do you want me to get my statement and read you the names?"

"Not right now," he says. "But thanks! I'll call you back for that." For the rest of the program little Bobbie was my most apt pupil.

Contacts who are old and far away may have the perfect tip for you to use in your search.

Even people you just met may have important career information for you. I had a client who was in a cab in Indianapolis riding to an interview, and decided to ask the cabbie about the company. "What do you think about _____ corp?" she asks.

"Oh, they're not a good company," he said. "I hear a lot of complaints about them. Tough place to work, unfair, broken promises. That kind of thing. I think _____ company is better, and they're in the same business."

She called up the other company and said, "Hey, I'm in town for an interview with your competitor, and I wonder if you'd have a moment to speak with me while I'm here on their dime."

She ended up getting an offer at both companies, and was able to choose the better one simply because she chatted up a cabbie on the way in from the airport.

This is why you don't hold back when making these lists. These weird connections are the norm, not the exception, in a job search. The apparently chaotic approach actually has a very high success rate. The reasons for this are the power of information is independent of the power of the source of that information, and information is mostly free. In most cases it does not require much of an introduction to get information. In short, the front door may be locked, but your most casual acquaintance may be able to walk you right in through the side door.

Remember, the social science researchers say you need to get past your closest friends to get the critical information you need. Your closest friends' friends, aka second-level contacts, are the portals into vast new worlds of information that you don't currently possess.

"Nothing succeeds like excess." —OSCAR WILDE

Your Online Communities

Contemporary Americans and Canadians are members of more online communities than they may realize. The two main types are professional communities and social communities, although frankly the line is blurring between the two. Both communities are a great source of leads for your lists. Check your participation or even passive observation in all the following:

Online professional networks. LinkedIn is becoming the main business networking service. Members expect to receive queries and commentaries of all types from colleagues in their network. Anyone in a job search should join LinkedIn if she is not already a member. Just for example, you can search for company names on LinkedIn and find groups for current, former, and prospective employees. Plaxo works like LinkedIn, and from what I can tell has a higher level membership (more attorneys and CFOs, fewer marketing assistants). New sites are popping up constantly, focusing on niches of all types.

Online social networks. Facebook was originally a purely social network, but it is becoming an "everything goes" network, with businesses of all types setting up Facebook listings, faculty connecting with students through this forum, clubs of all types using Facebook as a common space, and so on. Almost anyone in a job search should join Facebook if he is not already a member. MySpace works like Facebook, but has a generally younger crowd, and, for whatever reason, lots of musicians. Friendster is another option to explore. Again, new social sites focusing on specific affinity groups are popping up all the time.

Special interest groups (SIGs), blogs, listservs, news feeds (with a comment feature) related to your professional and personal interests. Whether its knitting or corporate HRIS, if you follow a blog or belong to a listserv or SIG, list that as an asset in your job search.

Associations have robust websites with member databases, and affiliated listservs, newsletters, Twitter accounts, and so on. **Alumni networks** are also associations. If you're a member, even passively, that's a listing. Whether you are young or old, a senior professional or just starting out in life, these networks are a *huge* asset in a job search. List all the associations you are a member of, and get on their lists for auto feed for news, information, and announcements. If you want to find more listservs and SIGs that might be pertinent to your professional life, explore www.asaecenter.org/Directories/AssociationSearch.cfm?navItemNumber=16581.

In short, you should be a member of at least one professional and one social online network. The more popular the network, the better. You should also activate and maximize your utilization of association-related online services. Other than that, you don't need to join a bunch of new sites. Depth is more important than breadth. Just be sure to list all the online social networks you participate in as you are building a map of the people who can help you find a job.

Throughout the book, when I write Facebook or LinkedIn or networking site, please remember that everything written there applies to your entire online world, from Twitter to your church's online newsletter. If you're really into these resources, check out *How to Find a Job on LinkedIn, Facebook, Twitter, MySpace and Other Social Networks* (McGraw Hill, 2010) and *I'm on LinkedIn—Now What???* (Happy About, 2009). If you don't understand any of this and want a primer for branding yourself online, Dan Schawbel's website has about a dozen; go to http://mashable.com/business/career-development. These social media resources are an integral part of HJM techniques, but never forget: you have to leave your house and meet people face to face to get a job.

Your IRL Communities

What communities of humans are you active with in real life (IRL)? Here are a few to consider listing:

Church, synagogue, mosque, ashram. That's possibly hundreds of people you're connected to IRL.

Volunteer organizations of any type, from the PTA to the American Red Cross to Habitat for Humanity. If you're an active member, list it.

Neighborhood watch, homeowners association, neighborhood business associations, basically any type of neighborhood-based organization. If they have meetings and you're entitled to attend, list them.

Gym, swim club, tennis club, country club. These are people with whom you have an existing connection.

Fraternal organizations from the Masons to E. Clampus Vitus to VFW. If you're a member, put it on the list.

Some communities confound a narrow definition because they bridge online and IRL worlds. **Alumni clubs, political parties, activist organizations** (such as Sierra Club) may have robust online and IRL communities, or they have a national online presence and a local IRL presence. You can list them in multiple categories.

Highly Productive Resources

You want to be highly systematic with the following categories of people. These are the contacts who are most likely to be helpful to you in your job search.

Former employers and colleagues. The people you've worked with and for need to be *systematically* and *comprehensively* listed. They know you in a work setting, and you have a connection with them even if you've not spoken to them in years. Include customers and clients and consultants and anyone else who qualifies. In the next chapter we'll talk about how to dust off your business network, but for now, just be diligent about recalling all your personal connections. And remember, you don't have to know their names! Your listings can be full of people like "that cute guy in the Milwaukee office" and "the European sales rep with the bad hair plugs." You can dig out actual names later.

Friends. Close friends. Old friends. New friends. Friends of friends. Colleagues. Acquaintances. Nodding acquaintances. People from the neighborhood. List them all. Friends are a deep and willing resource for your job search. Remember, your friends want you to be successful. Otherwise, they have to keep buying your drinks. So they're on your side.

Family. You have a big family, and you need to list them all. Any family member who could remember he ever met you. Don't leave out the old and retired; remember Aunt Ruthie! Family are predisposed to help you. They love you . . . and they don't want you to end up sleeping on their couch and scratching your butt in front of their fridge at two in the morning. Of course you always start with your mom, because your mom will take your call.

Friends of your family and **families of your friends.** This is a big secret: friends of your family and family of your friends are fantastic second-level contacts. Make lists of these people, as many as you know about now. You can poll your friends and family to get more later. These one-level-off contacts have a close connection on both sides of the social link, so they're very likely to be receptive to you, if you know how to approach them. "Destiny's cousin on Wall Street" may be the key to your next job.

Alumni. Alumni groups can be like cults. You can email someone with a twenty-year age difference, who lives in another city, and who is from a completely different socioeconomic world, and if you both went to the same college or university, suddenly she likes you. Alumni are a great resource! As mentioned in the prior section on associations, find out what you need to do to use the alumni database that every school has.

University career center, faculty, key university staff. Faculty and university staff have rich, invisible, national, and even international networks. They are connected to alumni, academic colleagues, and industry and government leaders all over. So, unless you graduated in the last millennium, list any faculty or staff who might remember you fondly or, even if they can't remember you, might have a network of value to you. *Everyone should contact his alma mater's career center even if he graduated fifty years ago.* That's a given. An absolute must.

Organizations That Want to Hire You

Now, let us turn to making lists of organizations that have the types of jobs you have targeted, whether you know anyone there or not, and whether they are currently hiring or not. First you need to describe likely employers as narrowly as possible, and then compile lists of *all* such employers in your search area. So if your target is public accounting, you'll want to find every CPA firm in your geographical area. If your target is to find a job as a safety and industrial hygiene officer in a chemical manufacturing plant, you'll need to find every chemical manufacturing plant within a commute of your desired locations.

To do a job search, you must do research. You probably do not already know the company or organization that will hire you.

Research leverages your job-search effort. If you go to the trouble to consider being a full-charge bookkeeper for one independent restaurant, why not apply to *all* the independent restaurants in your area? Once you learn the lingo for a particular type of job, it only makes sense to take that learning out on the road, get some mileage out of your effort. With every single restaurant owner that you talk to about being her full-charge bookkeeper, you'll gain more insider information, you'll become a better candidate, and you'll get closer to being hired.

Remember Aiden Spencer and his quest to become an income property manager? By looking for work *in a narrow channel,* he leveraged every contact in his very next interaction. So, you need to build lists of companies or nonprofits or elementary schools or whatever you have targeted that could hire you. Not random lists, mind you, but lists of the same *type* of organization that could hire you to do the same *specific* job.

This is both easy and hard. It's easy to get started, but it is hard to be totally systematic. You can use the yellow pages to find all the CPA firms in the downtown area, for example, but for the software development firms specializing in game development you're going to need more robust search tools.

First, let's define, as precisely as we can, the type of organization you are seeking. What is your vision of your next employer?

Industry, function, title. We already know these three words are the minimum definition of a job. (Revisit pages 24–26 if you don't remember what jobs you targeted.) The industry that a company is in can be defined by Standard Industry Classification (SIC) codes, which we'll explore in a moment. Function is what you will do all day. Title is just the name of the job, the handle by which the employer, and you, will refer to the job itself. Don't forget that you oughtn't go in more than three directions at a time, that is, it's not efficient to go after more than three types of job at the same time.

Location. You need to know what geographical parameters you will place on your search. "Anywhere in the U.S." is an acceptable answer. "Vancouver or Victoria" is an acceptable answer. "Inside my own zip code" is a great definition. "Within a thirty-minute commute of my home by public transportation" is another perfectly viable definition. Where are you going to look first?

Size of organization. Companies have traditionally been measured by annual revenues, number of employees, and total valuation. In a knowledge economy, total valuation is not as useful a measure as it was back in the big industrial days when locomotives were more important than brains, so let's concentrate on revenues and number of employees. Is your target a huge employer like Wal-Mart, the largest private employer in the world? Or is it a small owner-operated boutique with a handful of employees?

I have already established that in the United States, large organizations are net destroyers of jobs, smaller companies churn a lot of jobs, and mid-size companies are, in fact, the engine for permanent new job creation. So size is an important consideration in your job search. The definition of a "small business" or "mid-size business" is more complicated than you might think. About half the employees in the U.S. work for a company with fewer than 500 total staff. According to the U.S. Small Business Administration (SBA), 65 percent of new jobs are created by these businesses, and 35 percent are created by businesses with more than 500 employees. Don't over-interpret these data, however, as there is a huge difference between "new job" and "net new job." Other SBA data show "60 to 80 percent of net new jobs every year" come from small businesses.

The SBA calls many employers with 1 to 500 employees small businesses, but not all of them. For the SBA, business size is also a function of type of business. A very robust software development group or advertising agency might have only a few dozen employees, while a "small" chemical manufacturing plant might have as many as 1,000.

Another way to define mid-size businesses is to use the banking definition of **middle market** firms, that is, business establishments with $10 million to $500 million in annual revenues. To bankers, it's the money that counts. So, small markets would be organizations with $0 to $10 million in annual revenues, and large would be those companies with over $500 million annual revenues.

The Society for Human Resource Management (SHRM) generally cares more about employees than revenues. They often categorize businesses this way:

1. Small: 1 to 99 employees.
2. Medium: 100 to 499 employees.
3. Large: 500 and more employees.

There are millions of businesses, however, that better fit the category of **micro,** that is, they consist of the founder and one or two assistants. That's a distinctly different working environment than a company with ninety employees. More than half a million new businesses are started every year, and businesses with fewer than twenty workers generated 40 percent of job growth in the last recovery.

For our purposes, we'll adopt this rough taxonomy:

1. **Microbusiness:** probably owner operated, fewer than a dozen or so employees, and under a couple of million dollars or so in revenues per annum.

2. **Small business:** at most a few hundred employees, and a few million dollars in revenues per annum.

3. **Mid-size business:** roughly 100 to 1,000 employees, several millions of dollars in annual revenues, large enough to be stable yet small enough to be nimble.

4. **Large business:** more than 1,000 employees and at least several hundreds of millions of dollars in revenues per annum.

Considering all this, how big would you guess the organization is that you'd like to work for next? Micro, small, mid-size, or large?

Age. How old is the organization? Why would this matter? *The overwhelming majority of new jobs are created in new companies.* "According to the Census Bureau, nearly all net job creation in the

U.S. since 1980 occurred in firms less than five years old. . . . Put more starkly, without new businesses, job creation in the American economy would have been negative for many years" (*Wall Street Journal*, November 6, 2009, page A25).

Target new companies, less than five years old. (By the way, if you are a government official, learn where jobs really come from and build tax incentives around small businesses in your own community, not giant corporations based elsewhere.)

Structure of governance. Is it a public company, traded on a stock exchange and with extensive financial information readily available to anyone, or is it a privately held company, with financial information available only to officers of the company? This won't matter to most employees, but it is a parameter that you can specify if you have preference for one over the other.

Build job targets. Now, define your job idea in terms of industry, location, size in revenues, size in terms of employees, age, and, if it matters, structure of governance. Here are some models from actual job seekers participating in my workshops. None is a perfect definition, but all of them are a perfect place to begin!

- "I am looking for chemical manufacturing companies in New Jersey that are fewer than twenty-five years old, with more than $10 million in annual revenues and more than 100 employees. These are likely to be public companies, but I don't care if they are or not."

- "I am looking for a private high school in the Northeast where I can teach philosophy without a state teaching license. So, that's probably New England plus New York, New Jersey, and Pennsylvania. Boarding schools or day schools, either one would be fine."

- "I am looking for mining companies with locations in the West. I used to be a machinist for Ford, but those jobs are mostly gone now. Mines are one of the last big industries that use a lot of machinists in roles that can't be outplaced! So, I'm going to need a list of large, active mines in places like Arizona, Nevada, Wyoming, Texas, New Mexico, Montana, and Idaho, wherever there's active mining."

- "I am looking for smaller law firms within walking distance of my apartment in Clayton (an upscale commercial district of St. Louis). Ideally, I'd like to know every firm with at least five lawyers, but no more than fifty within the Clayton district."

- "I want to know the 100 largest paving and road contractors in Illinois that have been in business fewer than ten years. If the companies are young and large, I figure they're doing things right."

- "I want to know all the food manufacturing companies in the Inland Empire (a massive agricultural area east of Los Angeles). Every single one of them hires bilingual foremen like me."

Once you define your list, I'm going to give you a big tip: **you don't need to learn how to do research. You just need to learn how to ask for it!**

Here is a major source of assistance: **reference librarians.** If the last time you were in a library was in middle school, you're in for a big surprise. They're not just about books anymore. Libraries have become really cool media consulting centers, with everything from movies and art you can check out and take home to computer labs hooked up to every database in the world. Best of all, you can get real help there for your job search project. Some libraries even sponsor job clubs and job search training! So, get thee to the library.

You don't need to know how to find every graphic arts studio in Chicago; you just need to know how to walk into a library, find the reference librarian, *admit your ignorance and need for help,* and say something like this: "I'm a job seeker, and I need to build a list of possible employers in Chicago. I think graphic design and package design firms would be likely to hire me. Can you help me build a list of 100 graphic design studios or package design firms in the Loop?" The best time to hit the library for stuff like this is the moment it opens.

If one librarian is not helpful, try another. Go again at a different time. Go to a different branch. I'm not saying that every trip to the library is going to be fruitful, but when you get the right librarian, you've struck your own gold mine. Somewhere there's a librarian, waiting at a desk, eager for you to walk up and ask a question. The more precise, weird, arcane, or difficult the better. *They live for this kind of query.* Let them help you with research, so you can get on with the other stages of your job search.

College and university career centers also have research specialists on staff who live for queries like this. Career center research specialists will be versed in all the databases of companies and organizations, and can help you find lists like the ones specified above. If you ever attended a college or university, call them up and ask them about alumni services. Some charge a fee for support like this, and some do it for free. Either way, it's worth it.

Some **state employment development departments** and some **job clubs** have robust research support for job seekers. Some examples are Experience Unlimited, located in California, and Forty Plus, a nationwide club for professionals over forty. You should reach out to organizations like these anyway. Participation in job clubs can help you get the research support you need.

Finally, if you have enough money to hire some help with parts of your job search project, **information brokers** are independent research specialists who can find information for your job search in a matter of seconds. You can find information brokers who are members of the Association of Independent Information Professionals (AIIP) by going to www.aiip.org/MemberDirectory, and members of the Public Record Retrieval Network can be found at http://prrn.us. Also see www.nettrace.com.au/resource/search/info.html. A good information broker can be addictive, so watch your budget.

Information brokers, reference librarians, and research specialists can keep you from reinventing the wheel. They can keep you from doing research the hard way. For example, almost every licensed attorney in the United States is in the Martindale-Hubbell database, www.martindale.com/Find-Lawyers-and-Law-Firms.aspx. Almost every executive recruiter in the country (the best 13,000 of them) is in *The Directory of Executive & Professional Recruiters*, available in print and online versions from Kennedy Information, www.kennedyinfo.com. The U.S. headquarters of foreign companies can be found in *The Directory of Foreign Firms Operating in the United States* (Uniworld Business Publications, annual), available in the reference section of any library. These are just teasers for the types of information you can quickly and easily access.

If you want to do it yourself, here's how:

Online search. As mentioned earlier, start by searching online for your definition: "graphic arts in Chicago" or "transportation and logistics consultants in Los Angeles." This is a messy research method, but you should try it every single time. While you're at it, Google yourself and see if there are any naked pictures of you snorting cocaine floating around out there.

Online databanks. One of my favorite online resources is www.zapdata.com, which is a Dun & Bradstreet (D&B) portal with information on 14 million U.S. businesses. Basically, if an organization has a credit rating, it's in zapdata.com. I'll profile how zapdata.com works, and then mention some other portals that work similarly.

In zapdata, you can sort by type of business using SIC (Standard Industry Classification) codes. You can sort by size of company in terms of revenues or employees or both. You can sort for location by state, county, or even zip code, allowing you to find the companies nearest to your home to reduce your commute. You can look up a company's SIC code to find every other similar company. You can find secondary SIC codes, also. For example, maybe the company's main SIC code is management consulting, but it may have secondary SIC codes as a training and development contractor or a human resources consultancy.

If you pay a little extra, you can get name, phone number, and email contact information for a variety of company officers. You can learn if they export or import. You can find companies that have relocated to a new address, or that have just been formed or reformed legally, or that have just been reorganized in a spinoff or buyout. You can even specify that you want headquarter locations only, or branch locations only.

You can look for companies that are young, the chief job creators in our economy, even specifying that you want companies that are two to three years old, or four to five years old, or, probably best of all, two to five years old. These tools are so amazing; once you learn how to use them you can even find the nearest B&B to your Aunt Ruthie's house in Florida!

The data are cheap enough for most people. With zapdata in particular you can buy information for one company or a million; you can even preview up to fifty companies at a time for free.

Other tools that work similarly to www.zapdata.com are www.hoovers.com/free, www.google.com/Top/Business, and www.referenceUSA.com. Hoovers is also a D&B company, based ultimately on the same data, and many consider its portal easier to use than zapdata's. ReferenceUSA is a branch of InfoUSA, and claims to have company records on 10.5 million U.S. businesses, and more than 1 million Canadian businesses. Here's a really big tip: universities and libraries often have master agreements with these data portals, so you may not have to pay a dime for data if you have a library card or university career center privileges! Finally, Dun & Bradstreet has a different business search site: http://dnb.powerprofiles.com. It's stripped down but easier to use. A lot of my clients find this portal provides sufficient information to build local lead lists, and it's free. Don't spend a lot of money on any of these sites until you compare several of them. Some combination of free features may get you all the information you need.

Again, it all boils down to how precise your list design is in the first place. "I'm looking for every modeling and talent agency in Nebraska" is a good query. "I'm looking for green companies" is not refined enough to use these types of research tools, although somewhere there is a reference librarian hoping that someone walks up to his desk and says, "I want to work for a green company. How would I find or create a list of them?"

Yellow pages. Yes, they still print them and, yes, they're still useful. They're better for finding consumer-focused businesses, like auto body shops, than they are for finding business-to-business organizations, like software integration consultants.

Business journal lists. Print business journals still exist in most metro areas, and one of the hallmarks of these publications is their weekly lists. They'll have lists of the largest employers, the largest insurance companies, the largest law firms, and so on, ad infinitum. Check their websites.

Chambers of commerce. Check the websites for your local chamber of commerce. They publish all kinds of data, almost always free, and almost always available right off their websites.

Business licenses. Business licenses are now often available through government websites. You can go through businesses formed over the last two years to look for young companies that are growing.

Commercial real estate sales, leasing notices. Commercial real estate transactions are a particularly robust way to discover new jobs. A company putting in a new location, or moving to a new location, is always going to have staffing needs.

Associations. As I've mentioned, associations are a great data resource for job seekers. Associations generally focus on individual members, and the overwhelming majority of those members will be employed. Every one of those employers is a potential lead for you. Associations also have institutional members, and you may be able to access those lists.

Employment websites, consolidators, career portals. This is where the majority of job seekers spend the majority of their time, and where you should spend as little time as possible. If you're interested in a company, go to *its* employment website. Even then, you're getting involved in the job creation process late, after a position has been posted. Nevertheless, here are some of the top career websites: www.monster.com, http://hotjobs.yahoo.com, www.job.com, www.careerbuilder.com, www.jobbankusa.com, and dozens more I'll tell you how to find in just a moment. (This list is just a starting point.)

Consolidators are online sites that research multiple sites and alert you to jobs that match your interests. Although, frankly, many of the really large portals listed above are starting to do this too, so this distinction may disappear. Here are some of the main consolidator sites at the time this book went to press: www.simply hired.com, www.indeed.com, www.hound.com, and www.alljob search.com. There are many, many more.

For executives, I like CareerJournal, the *Wall Street Journal*'s career website, which has moved to http://online.wsj.com/public/page/news-career-jobs.html, and the new *Wall Street Journal* portal for financial jobs, FINS.com, as well as www.execunet.com, www.theladders.com, and www.6figurejobs.com. Some of these charge fees, yet the articles and high-quality advice on these sites may well be worth a subscription fee.

Other specialty sites cover certain industries, like www.dice.com for tech jobs or www.higheredjobs.com for university employment or www.healthcarejobs.com, which is for, I dunno, healthcare jobs? Not to be confused with http://healthcare.jobs.com, or www.health-care-jobs.com, or www.allhealthcarejobs.com, and many similar others.

Finally, there are sites that specialize in certain parts of the country.

To find all the job sites on the Web that matter to you, go to Peter Weddle's *Weddle's 2009/10 Guide to Employment Sites on the Internet* (Weddle's, 2009), the definitive guide. This book is in every library in the English-speaking areas of North America, so you can go check it out in the nearest library to see if there is a website dedicated to your region, level, or functional expertise.

Anyone engaged in a job search should spend a little bit of time on such sites, but that's it. You can spend twenty-four hours a day on these sites if you want, but if that's still your desire just throw this book out the nearest window.

Your Goal Is 100 Leads

You need to keep 100 leads going at all times in your job search. Your raw leads will be a mix of items—some people, some organizations, some ideas to pursue—but the total should always add up to or exceed 100.

If you can't find 100 leads in a particular direction—say, modeling and talent agencies in Nebraska—then you've got to reconsider your goal.

Remember, no amount of effort will magically increase the number of employers that match your search criteria. If you can't find enough employers, your search criteria will need to be revised. Either consider a wider range of jobs, or consider moving out of Four Corners, Nowhere, to reach your career objectives.

In some cases, a person will have a very limited universe of organizations that she is considering. To reach 100 leads she will have to have lots of individual *people* at those organizations. No one gets a pass on the 100 minimum leads rule. In general, the hidden job market system works if you look for a certain type of job, not if you look only at working at a specific employer.

As leads fall away, you'll have to replace them. You'll come back to this chapter as your search progresses, to make sure you're being systematic, and following every lead. Your marketing campaign will have phases. You'll pursue one direction for a while—say, all the members of a professional association—then pursue another direction for a while, for example, all the iterations of a certain type of employer.

As your search progresses, you'll consume leads. You may discover you have no connections at Really Cool Company and, after sending a few emails to them and applying online, they're not really an ongoing "active item" for you. Really Cool Company can go deep into a six-month tickle file and you'll need to turn to one of your ninety-nine-plus other options to keep advancing in your search. You may find that your rich uncle is an ass—and he's not going to help you find a job. So you'll have to turn to your ninety-nine-plus other contacts to seek help toward your next job.

Deciding when an active item is no longer active is a matter of judgment. If you can think of one more link to an insider at the company, then it's still active, and your task is to explore that link. If you are under consideration for a position and they have not yet dinged you, then it's still active. But if you can't think of anything more to do to get a job there, then push it over into the inactive file and start working on another idea.

In chapters 7, 8, 9, and 10, we'll talk about how to approach people and get them to help you, and how to approach organizations and get the *people* in those organizations to help you, too. But first let's turn to how to keep all this information organized.

6

MANAGING HUNDREDS OF LEADS

The Organizational Challenge of Managing Hundreds of Leads

You're soon going to find that you have hundreds of leads to track and manage. I don't care how you do it, but be ready to be effective at it. You'll need to know when you last contacted an organization or person, and what you said or sent her. You'll need a tickle system that lets you know when you should contact her next. You'll need to manage individual people, like your Aunt Ruthie; whole groups of people, such as your alumni association; and individual organizations that may contain thousands of people, for example a company you've identified as a preferred employer.

Here are some ways job seekers deal with these details (people, companies, appointments, calendars, reminders, and so on):

Online job-seeker sites such as JibberJobber, careerfitness, and similar. These act as an electronic filing cabinet for job seekers. There's no need to reinvent the wheel, but I do want to warn you that you'll be spending a lot of your time uploading information and keeping all your information current. This can be a time suck, but if your search is long, it'll be worth it. You have to manage this data one way or another anyway, so you're going to be investing quite a bit of time in the process no matter which media you use.

Lists. Lists are a fine way of managing information, and it doesn't matter whether your lists are on paper or on your computer in Word or in Excel. If you put them in Excel you can sort them easier in multiple categories, but if you're not a strong Excel user you'll spend more time trying to make the program work than making your job search work. One advantage: the lists are yours—until your computer fails. So be sure to back up regularly.

Cards. Some people still use 3 x 5 or 5 x 8 cards to manage their contacts. The advantage of this system is that the cards can be sorted by date of next activity. They are a paper-based tickle system. If you're not computer savvy, or just not that into learning new applications, this is definitely the best system to use. For several thousand years (more or less) those little white cards were the norm for business and school notes, so why get fancy now?

Cards are also a good system to augment your more sophisticated databases, to keep up with information as you acquire it in real time, and before you transfer it to something more agile.

Appointment ledger. This is super obvious, but you need an appointment book, whether it's on your computer or in your purse. Most business computers have more than one freebie appointment and calendar system already on them, such as Microsoft Works Calendar. There are online systems as well, such as www.appointment-plus.com, www.clickbook.com, and www.genbook.com. It doesn't matter which you use as long as you use it religiously. If someone says, "Call me in three months," you'd better be able to make sure you call him in exactly ninety days.

CRM tools. Major corporations invest millions in CRM applications. CRM stands for Customer Relationship Management. Some programs designed for individual use include ACT, available at www.act.com; SalesForce, available at www.salesforce.com/CRM; http://highrisehq.com, with a 30-day free trial; or GoldMine, available at www.frontrange.com/goldmine.aspx or wherever fine software is sold. If you are not familiar with contact management software, this is probably overkill to attempt to learn it now; just go with JibberJobber or careerfitness or similar. On the other hand, if you have used CRM at work and liked it, the cost of some of these is quite reasonable considering the power and the features. Email management systems like iContact or ConstantContact, designed for small business use, can also be utilized in a job search if you want to get serious about running a large, sophisticated search for your next job. They are robust email tools, not full CRM tools, but they may fit your needs.

Again, there's no wrong way to manage your data—except poorly. In practice, you'll probably have some combination of several media, some data that live on your computer, some kind of CRM-like data management system, some lists that you access off of other people's systems (such as an alumni database), and some random notes and cards in every pocket of your suit. You can move up to more robust applications when your existing systems fail to provide the support you need.

Remember that you will have hundreds of contacts and details to manage, and you need to be precise, systematic, and unfailingly accurate to successfully crack the hidden job market.

7

HOW TO REACH OUT TO PEOPLE

People Want to Help You

I have very good news for you: people want to help you. They actually want to assist you in your job search. But, they can only help you if you approach them correctly, if you'll help them help you. You can't go down your contact list begging for a job. In fact, that's the worst way to use—and I do mean "use"—your contacts. You can't ask them to tell you who you are and what you want. You can't ask them to buy you coffee or drinks or dinner and listen to your woes. So, how do you help them help you? By knowing what you want precisely enough that they can provide information to advance your search.

Rule #1: Stop asking for a job. That's right. Do not ask people for a job or for a job at their company. You'll get a job faster by asking for information, rather than for a job. When you ask people for a job, you force them into the unhappy position of having to say "no" to you. No one wants to say no. It makes them uncomfortable. But everyone is happy to give you advice and information. It makes them feel good. They want to help you, and you're helping them feel good by letting them help you in your search. Ask for information, not a job.

Rule #2: Ask about a very precise career goal. Your request must be precise or people won't know what information would be useful to you. For example, don't ask for information about "green jobs." That's too vague, too broad. Ask what they might know about the large-scale wind turbine farms that are popping up all over the country. Then let the conversation go on to small-scale wind turbines, green buildings, geothermal power generation, and what have you. *Start with a very narrow and precise query.*

Rule #3: Avoid "yes" or "no" questions. Whenever possible, favor open-ended queries. Yes-or-no questions limit the range of responses, and stifle creativity. Asking open-ended questions allows your respondent to help you in ways that you could not have foreseen: Here's an example: "I am interested in internships at the

United Nations. Who do you know who would know anything about internships at the United Nations?"

Rule #4: Assume each and every contact has some gem of information for you. Remember Aunt Ruthie from Florida! Remember Dee the dog walker! Some years ago, I led a university workshop in rural Georgia and we were playing the networking game. In the networking game, a job seeker stands up in a group and says, "Who do you know who would know anything about _____?" That day a student stood up and said, "Who do you know who would know anything about being a casting director or a talent agent?" I was just thinking that rural Georgia was a long way from Hollywood when a student volunteered, "My aunt is a casting director in Santa Monica." Boom. Just like that. Expect wild connections, because they are common.

Rule #5: Contacting people is about information, not power. You want to talk to people who will give you good advice, leads, and referrals. You need people with information on your contact lists, and they don't need to be powerful at all. This is an important concept to understand, because many job seekers seem to want to approach powerful people. Powerful people can decide to hire you, which is the attraction, of course. But people with information lead you to the people who can hire you. Powerful people are actually hard to access, and may know little or nothing of value to you in your search. The best contact of all is someone who right now has the job you want next, someone who is two to five years ahead of you. That's someone who can tell you the secret knock that gets you in the door.

It's great if someone has both the power to help you and useful knowledge for your job search, but in general, always favor information over power. Janitors and mechanics and receptionists can give you the critical tip you need to find your next career opportunity. We'll talk about a sponsored mailing later, which is one case where information and power come into play simultaneously. For now, just don't worry about power at all.

Instead, follow these rules for contacting people in your job search:

1. **Don't ask them for a job.**

2. **Know precisely what job you're curious about.**

3. **Favor open-ended questions; avoid yes-or-no queries.**

4. **Assume everyone has some information that will be useful to you somehow.**

5. **Remember that you want to connect to people with information, whether or not they have any power.**

Start by Dividing Your Universe of Contacts into Four Categories

Okay, so you know 600 to 10,000 people, and you've started to build lists of all of them. Where do you start if you're now going to contact them? Start by dividing them into these four categories:

- Hiring Authorities
- Direct Referral Sources
- Centers of Influence
- Everyone Else

Hiring authorities. These are people in the right industry who are in a position of sufficient power to hire you if they decided to do so. If they like you they could hire you, end of story. The quintessential hiring authority is someone who would be your direct boss if you were to join that specific company. Hiring authorities can also be further up the ladder. This is the classic "rich uncle" who owns a company. This is anyone, whether you have any connection with him or not, who would be in a position to hire you if he wanted to do so.

As a warning, though, hiring has become much more formulaic in the past couple of decades. Rich uncles are much less likely to override the opinions of their HR staff than they used to be. And even CEO's nieces are routinely told, "Gosh, it's great that you know the CEO, but we just don't have a match for your skill set right now." Someone powerful deciding to "just put you on the payroll" or "find *something* for you to do" is more of a myth than a common practice. So concentrate on line managers who would directly supervise you.

Direct referral sources. These are people in the right industry, but who are not themselves hiring authorities. These are people who can refer you to hiring authorities in one or two steps.

These are the people who can tell you who's hiring, who's not, how to get hired, when people hire, the magic words to say, and so on. These are also the people who have the exact job you want next. You'll want to spend as much time as you can with direct referral sources. They'll be your best resources for advice, ideas, leads, and referrals. In short, anyone you can find in the industry you have targeted can be a direct referral source for you.

In the formula for career success, which you learned about in chapter 3, step two is *always* a direct referral source:

1. Identify a job target of interest.

2. Find someone doing that job *right now*.

3. Talk to him/her.

4. Repeat until hired.

Centers of influence, also known as connectors, boundary spanners, and mavens. Centers of influence are people who by nature of position or personality just know a lot of people, or share a lot of information across organizational lines, or have tons of "followers" who will be guided by their tastes, style, and consumer decisions. Social networking has codified these people into businesses such as Angie's List or Craigslist, but the phenomenon is cultural, not technological, and certainly predates the Internet.

In terms of job search, centers of influence have access to information that may be of great value to you. Interestingly enough, centers of influence often have no structural authority, even though they may have tons of suasion power. Secretaries are often centers of influence. They know how to operate within the culture of an organization. They know which departments are favored, and which are a dead end, and which will be the first to suffer if layoffs start.

Centers of influence are often boundary spanners, people who exist within one organization but have connections into many, many others. Salespeople, consultants, attorneys, accountants, hairdressers, gossips, aficionados, bartenders (in the right bars), dog walkers, receptionists, recruiters, and taxi drivers are all boundary spanners. Their value to you is clear: they have information on lots of organizations, and they can see trends that should influence your decisions as you develop and refine your job-search goals.

Finally, in everyday practice, centers of influence are those sometimes annoying people who seem to always be forwarding you funny emails. If you have blocked these senders due to the steady stream of information, now would be a great time to resubscribe. These people are powerful information brokers. They're connected, often, to thousands of other people, and if you can enlist them in your efforts, they can gain you access to information and people that can make a difference in your search. Of course, the traffickers in political diatribes and the low-brow humor may have limited potential to introduce you to your next employer, but every industry, from advertising to zymurgy, has online mavens who pass along all kinds of industry gossip, rumors, insider jokes, and so on. You should think long and hard about whether you know or can access any of these online superconnectors.

Everyone else. And I do mean *everyone* else. Including Aunt Ruthie and your creepy Uncle Bob and the people in line with you as you get your morning coffee. You'll get a lot of false positives from the J. Random Public, but you'll also get connections such as the ones I've mentioned often in this book. A false positive is when people try to help you, genuinely, but they are just completely off base. There's always some acquaintance who thinks he knows someone who can hook you up with an opportunity, but it turns out to be an opportunity to join a multilevel marketing scheme. Or they say they know someone on Wall Street, and when you chase down that lead it turns out it's some third cousin with a newsstand near Wall and Broad.

In groups you can easily play the networking game, where a job seeker gets up and asks something like, "Who knows anyone who works for a Republican politician in a staff role, or works on political campaigns?" If you get a group of fifty or more, most players will get a hit of some kind. But you don't really need fifty people in a room to have the same hit rate. You can simply ask fifty people *sequentially*, "Who do you know who would know anything about _____?" This should be your habit for the duration of your job search.

Now that you have your categories of contacts, you'll set about systematically letting everyone in all four categories know that you're looking for work. Announce to the world that you are unemployed and exactly what kind of position you're interested in finding next. There is zero stigma attached to unemployment anymore. No one will think less of you for being "on the market." They'll think less of you for not doing something about it, for watching hours and hours of daytime TV, and indulging yourself in self-pity. But the fact that you need a job is no longer socially compromising.

Your job is to market yourself. Marketing is about projecting and collecting information. Do not hide under a barrel, but proclaim it from the rooftops!

Triage

There are only so many hours in the day, and you're only going to use about forty of them a week to look for work. So you need a system to allocate your efforts. That's triage. You want to put your greatest effort into the highest potential return areas. Talking to people you interact with casually, from cab drivers to hairdressers to telephone solicitors, is just easy and available. To use a business cliché, it's low-hanging fruit. Of course you'll do that. Besides, it works. On the other hand, structuring your approach to contacting hundreds of people who know you in various contexts of your life requires a bit more planning.

You get jobs by talking to people, so your goal is to talk to a lot of people. Email counts as "talking to people" as long as there is an exchange of useful information. Talking on the phone counts. Videoconferencing with VOiP on your laptop counts. Meeting for coffee or lunch counts. Meeting to ask someone questions about his job or industry counts. Meeting to interview for a "possible" current or future opening is best of all. One type of talking leads to the next.

Ironically, it's not always best to start with hiring authorities! There are only so many of them in the world, they're hard to access, and you're probably only going to get one chance to impress them. Where to start instead? Start by talking to people who currently hold the job you want next. They'll tell you how one can actually get hired into that role. Don't avoid a hiring authority if you stumble across one, of course, but don't systematically target them until you're sure of your direction.

Here's a really big warning: **if you can't get people who currently hold the position you desire to talk to you, you can't get that job anyway.** That's a startling statement, but it's absolutely true.

Magical thinking is rampant among job seekers. Here are some cases from my own experience: Someone who'd never sold a car in his life wanted to be a dealership sales manager in charge of a staff of fifty and an advertising budget of over $1 million. A student in a workshop told me she wanted to be a radiologist, but didn't even know what the word meant, and didn't know that it involved going to medical school. Another workshop attendant wanted to be a chef, but had never been a cook and as far as I could ascertain, knew nothing about good food or fine dining. Another wanted to be an FBI agent, but quickly disclosed that he had a felony arrest for drug dealing. That's all magical thinking.

Why is talking to people so valuable? It's because people want to help you. And sometimes that help is to send you in a new direction, away from something that's impossible, unlikely, or ultimately undesirable *for you*. This is called career exploration, and this is why you don't start by talking to hiring authorities. Hiring authorities who might be very impressed by you once you've talked to some other people first, may want to throw you out of their office if they're the first person you've met in this field. Remember Aiden Spencer? He talked to a lot of people before impressing the property manager who hired him.

When you talk to people they'll tell you little things that can make a big difference. Aiden's process of discovery was very typical. No one told him any one thing that fundamentally changed his ability to perform in the job he had targeted. But all the little tips he had accumulated made him walk and talk like a property manager. As the saying goes, if it walks like a duck and quacks like a duck, it must be a property manager.

Start your HJM search by contacting a particular subset of direct referral sources. Remember, direct referral sources are people who are in the right industry, but are not themselves hiring authorities. The highest priority for you is to talk to people in the industry you have targeted *who are currently doing the job you want next.*

Here's your triage:

- First objective: Talk to people who hold the job you want next.

- Second objective: Talk to as many direct referral sources as you can.

- Third objective: Talk to centers of influence to see if they can guide you to people who match your first and secondary objectives.

- Fourth objective: Activate your entire universe of possible contacts to try to get more information on direct referral sources and hiring authorities.

- Final objective: Talk to hiring authorities when it happens naturally and, later, when you know you are ready to get that job, when you can walk and talk like a duck.

Most people are happy to provide advice to someone who knows how to ask for it, and that's what you're going to do.

Here's an interesting and important point: you are not using a request for advice as a subterfuge to gain access to people. You're asking for advice because you genuinely need it. So this is not a trick. It's a legitimate process of discovery.

If the company is hiring and you'd be appropriate for a position, your contact will bring it up. If they're hiring for a position for which you'd be perfect and they don't bring it up, then they don't like you anyway. Or at least they don't like you for that position. Trust this process.

When People Know You: Get to the Point

If people know you, you don't have to introduce yourself. If you're after information, state what information is needed and what you want to have happen next. Again, avoid asking yes-or-no questions, and do ask for advice, ideas, leads, and referrals.

Here's a perfectly serviceable formula to follow when writing to people who know you: Why you're writing. What you want. What should happen next. Bing. Bang. Boom. That's it.

Here are two examples:

Chrissy,

Hey, I guess you heard. I got the ax! They're closing down the marketing department for Cape Canaveral Microbrew. I told them that
expanding was a dumb idea! That's why they call it "micro" brew.
Duh! I think they were sampling too much of their own product
when they made that decision.

Anyway, on into the future. Say, could you help me out with my job
search? I'm not looking for a position with your company. I'm just
wondering who else you know in marketing or the advertising world,
or even in food and beverage. Can I give you a ring to see if you
have advice, ideas, leads, or referrals for me? What's a good time
to connect?

Standing by,
Martine D'Aubaussie

Martine is a bit casual, and he breaks the rule that you should
never criticize a former employer, but this kind of quick personal
note is just fine for close friends. Compare with this:

Attn: Nanci Pearson
Re: Corporate Training & Development

Nanci, it was great to see you at the ASTD meeting last night. As I
mentioned to you briefly, I've decided to look around a bit for a new
opportunity. My current employer, Sisyphus Corp, certainly seems to
be doing fine, but program rollout is glacial. We just keep doing the
same old thing, over and over. I'd be interested in a more dynamic
environment.

My areas of professional interest include management and executive soft skills development, cross-cultural team development,
and design of CBT modules for on-demand distribution (mainly via
intranet at Sisyphus).

I'm wondering if you've heard anything about innovation in these
areas. I'd like to have a brief telephone conversation with you,
explain what I'm looking for, and see what advice or ideas you may

have for me. I'm not looking for a position with your company; I think you're one of those people who seems to know everybody and what they're up to. Do you have time to connect by phone, or do you have any tips you can provide via email? Let me know what's best.

Standing by,
Zen Petri

Call to Action

One of the most important parts of any communiqué is the call to action. What do you want to happen next? Be very clear you are not asking them for a job, or even help to find a job with their company, if you want a higher response rate.

A call to action is usually at the bottom of a cover letter or an email. Be precise about what it is you're seeking. Either you're looking for information by return email: "Who do you know who would know anything about becoming a personal trainer in Wisconsin?" or you're looking to connect by phone, or meet for coffee, or have a brief conversation to get that specific information.

So what do you want? Do you want them to email you information? Do you want them to call you? Accept a call *from* you? Keep an ear open for any news that might help you? Introduce you to their friend Melinda? People can't help you if they don't know what you want.

Here's an example: "I'll ring you tomorrow before noon. I hope you'll have a moment for a brief chat. And I wonder if you could remind me of your friend's name in Chicago that started that bakery."

Watch out for sounding like a whiner or a time suck. Sound excited. You're moving forward. Sound curious. Anything but depressed and depressing. Be thoughtful about word choice. All words have emotive impact, in addition to their literal meaning. Avoid the word "interview." Don't ask to "interview" someone or to be "interviewed" by someone. Interviews are a hassle and take a lot of time. Use wording like "chat" or "quick conversation," or "trade some gossip." That sounds like something almost anyone could afford.

In a call to action, avoid that old saw "If I don't hear from you within ten days, I'll follow up by phone." Business and social worlds move at lightning speed, now. Ten days equals "forever." My rough estimate of the attention span of a contact right now is one to two days, max. If they don't respond by the end of tomorrow, they're very likely not going to respond ever. So, if you mention a timeline or deadline, keep it very proximate.

Ditch That Resume!

Do not send a resume when networking in a job search. This is counterintuitive, and different from the advice in many other job-search guides. *Provide a resume only when requested.* Otherwise, don't send it. When people see a resume, they are programmed to delete it or send it on to HR, which amounts to the same thing. Also, when people see a resume, they assume you want a job in their company. This forces them into that uncomfortable role of telling you they can't help you.

I've written three books on how to write resumes, and I think resumes are fascinating, powerful documents. You'd think if anyone had a bias in favor of resumes, it would be me. But the truth is that resumes impede networking for information! Provide one promptly when requested by a contact but, otherwise, leave that sword in its scabbard. People don't like resumes, but they do like to be helpful and to provide advice. So ask for advice, and withhold the resume until the appropriate time.

Of course you need to get a few trusted friends and colleagues to read and review your resume, but that is different from sending it to the overwhelming majority of your contacts, where you will be seeking "advice, ideas, leads, and referrals."

The Right Way to Send a Resume

Websites and HR people will give you clear instructions on how to submit resumes to them. Follow those instructions! The most common and universally accepted way to submit a resume to an employer is as an attachment in Word (.doc or .docx) or Adobe (.pdf). Anyone requesting your resume will expect you to be able to submit it in one of these formats.

For more on how to handle resumes, be sure to see my guide, *The Overnight Resume: The Fastest Way to Your Next Job* (Ten Speed Press, 2010).

Job Blogs or Tweets Can Be Great, but Avoid Mass Mailings

You can post your queries on LinkedIn and on Facebook and on list-servs, of course, but most of your networking efforts will be one-to-one emails. Avoid mass mailings to email lists. It may be appealing to put 100 people on some CC group and send out "Dear Friends & Colleagues—" emails, but these have *vastly* lower response rates and are a waste of your network. If people are worthy of your inquiry, they are worthy of your asking them, individually, for their help.

I know it is laborious to repeatedly send the same query to dozens and dozens of people, but if you want them to help you, you will do it. There are some mail managers who can automate this process, like iContact or ConstantContact. These services allow you to customize email blasts so that they appear to your recipients as one-to-one emails. You can always copy and paste and customize yourself. You have to show some interest in your contacts as individuals, if you want them to give you help as an individual. Remember, you have to eat up forty hours a week on job search anyway, so you may as well relax and get ready for some repetitive work.

Some job seekers have set up blogs to give a daily, blow-by-blow account of their job search. You have two choices: One is to build a blog to support your search, using your real name. That's fine as long as you're hyper-aware that potential employers may read every word of it before you get to the hiring stage. I've seen this done with great effect, in particular in creative areas like writing or fashion design.

Second, you could build a blog with a different purpose: to release your frustrations. In this case, you'd better invent a fake name and persona. We all know that most employers are going to go looking for your online footprint. I've seen some fascinating and hilarious and horrific blogs detailing frustrations of the search, weird interviews and weird interviewers the job seeker has endured, and heinous treatment from employers. It is very much my recommendation that you resist the temptation to go in this direction unless you are veiled behind an anonymous front.

Twitter is an interesting medium to use in a job search. For one thing, companies are making a presence there and perusing user profiles looking for employees. And if you already have a Twitter following, then of course you can tweet them about your nervousness going into an interview, or tweet them with queries, such as "I just found out Martine was fired from Cape Canaveral! Anyone know the marketing manager there????"

Spell Check, Proofread, Look Stuff Up

For the duration of your job search, your emails and letters are an example of the type of work you would do for an employer. If your contacts get emails with silly emoticons, txt spellings, and errors in them, they are going to be reluctant to share leads with you. They will be reluctant to vouch for you, or let you use their names as a referral. It is not enough to use spell-check, by the way. You will need to engage your brain, to see if the words are used correctly, not just spelled correctly. Their are five misteaks in this sentence, misteaks that any manger should fine. You'll need to look up the correct spelling of words that are not in any dictionary, like company names, and the proper names of products, software, geographical locations, and so on.

The careful use of language is not just a sign of a good education; it is considered a sign of intelligence. Don't let anyone think you're not all that bright because you skip proofreading.

Thirty-Second Introduction, aka an "Elevator Speech"

For people who don't know you well, you will want to condense your situation into a one-paragraph narrative that can be used in an email or said aloud in a telephone call or even a social setting. The classic version of this piece of personal branding is known as an elevator speech. Suppose you stepped onto an elevator and glanced over at the ID badge of the person next to you, and it read "VIP." Maybe the person is the CEO of the company you work for, or want to work for. What could you say in the brief time you are together that could change your life, and hers? That's an elevator speech.

Originally designed for phone calls, most elevator speeches now come in the form of an initial email. Here are two examples:

I am a college student majoring in psychology. I am interested in sports administration. I am on several campus committees devoted to promoting and producing sporting events, both intercollegiate and intramural. My ultimate goal would be to land in sports marketing and sponsorship sales, but I am also interested in other areas. I got your name from the alumni office, and I wonder if you would have a moment to speak with me about the sports business.

My name is Madison Marten. I got your name from the Global Logistics Association member list, and I wonder if you would have a moment to speak with me about your own career. I am looking for an opportunity in operations management. My experience to date has emphasized matrix- and liaison-management of offshore manufacturing plants, working with both joint-venture/contracting structures and wholly owned offshore units. I speak Spanish fluently, and have picked up a little Chinese and Gaelic. My career interest is global manufacturing and anything to do with synchronization of non-co-located corporate operations, such as engineering on one continent and production on another. I'm calling because I understand your company has operations in Taiwan. I am not necessarily looking for a position with your company, but I am interested in getting your advice. Would you have a moment to chat with me by phone?

Explain (a) who you are, (b) how you know them, (c) why you're contacting them, and (d) what you want to happen next. Be straightforward, be direct, and remember to push hard for referrals, people you can talk to next. Broken down, here is the skeleton of a typical script for a thirty-second introduction:

Hello, _____. My name is _____. I was referred to you by _____. I'm interested in learning more about _____. I wonder if you would have a moment to share with me any advice, ideas, leads, and referrals.

You should construct your own thirty-second introduction right now. Write it out, then read it aloud to see if it has a good flow. Remember to convey who you are, why you are calling or emailing, and what you want.

Connecting in the Multimedia World: Research → Email → Call or Visit

The best way to contact people, even casual friends, is to research them a bit online. Make sure you have an accurate email address for them. Make sure they still work for the company you think they do. Check out their Facebook page and LinkedIn profile and see whether they're still married, still live in Connecticut, still appear to be sane, have any new tattoos, etc.

Then, email them your networking query or thirty-second introduction. Be clear in your call to action about what you want to happen next. Your goal for almost everyone who is in the industry you have targeted is to have a telephone conversation or an eyeball-to-eyeball meeting. Whether they're a hiring authority or the third assistant night security guard, you want to talk to them. If you're in Miami and they're in Boston, obviously this is going to be a phone call, but if you're both in San Francisco you want to get as much face time as possible. "Out of sight out of mind" is a cliché for a reason: because it's true. Circulate. Let people see you. Dress up for lunch meetings as if you, also, were working downtown.

For centers of influence, I also recommend a phone call if you can get them to speak with you. Have a fuller conversation about what you're after, what information you'd consider pertinent, and what you would be delighted to discover.

For everyone else, polling them by email is a good enough test of whether they can help you. You don't want to be having coffee for coffee's sake. Save your face time for people with a high probability of being able to give you a useful tip, lead, or referral.

The Three-Shot Email System

Email three times, minimum. If you are willing to email people once, you should be willing to email them at least three times, using the three-shot system.

People are busy. They are multitasking. They have family obligations. They may be traveling. They may be accessing their email across multiple platforms. They aren't always sure which emails they've read yet. Some people prefer Facebook to email, and consider all email to be spam, and you have to poke them to reach them at all. Others have several email accounts, one for work, one for dating, another for e-commerce. Some have security settings so high their mom can't reach them. Others receive a couple hundred emails a day, and sort them really fast, maybe on a train or in a meeting or while otherwise distracted. Some people check all their accounts daily, and some busy people haven't looked at LinkedIn or Plaxo in a month, and so on.

It's easy to miss an email! Therefore, when people don't respond to your email, it doesn't mean they don't love you. It may mean that they haven't even seen your query at all.

Again, if you are willing to email people once, you should be willing to employ the three-shot system: (1) Email them. (2) If they don't respond to that email, three days after you send it, *send the exact same missive again.* Exact same, no changes at all. Assume they're busy, and just overlooked your query in the everlasting waterfall of incoming emails. (3) If they don't respond to that second email, four days after that send the same email, but with a new top on it: "Dear Dr. Wilson—I'm not sure I have an accurate email address for you. What follows is what I've been trying to find out last week and this. I'd be truly grateful if you'd have even a moment to respond." Then put the original email below that. Perfectly polite.

THE THREE-SHOT SYSTEM

1. Email them.

2. If no response, wait three days, and email them again.

3. If no response, wait four days and put a new top on the email, "Dr. Wilson, I may not have an accurate email address for you . . . "

If they don't respond to any of these, then assume you have a bad email address. Find another email address, or approach them on Facebook and do the whole thing in that medium, or on Plaxo or LinkedIn. Never whine, but be persistent. *Follow the process to its conclusion.* If they don't respond to any of these attempts, and you really want to reach them, reformat the email into a standard business letter and mail it to them the old-fashioned way. If they ignore that, game over. Scratch their names from your lists. Invoke the old Yiddish curse: "You are dead to me."

None of this is too aggressive. I could teach you "too aggressive," but this is just one busy professional trying to reach another in the modern multimedia world.

When You Should Worry about Being "Too Aggressive"

Most job seekers seem to be constantly afraid of being overly aggressive. However, most aren't even close to being aggressive at all, much less overly aggressive. Most err on the side of being too timid. And there's a difference between looking for opportunity and being under consideration for a position. If you're looking for information, there's almost no limit to acceptable practice. However, if you're a finalist in a hiring process, calling over and over crosses some kind of line of civility and decorum.

In more than twenty years of working with job seekers, I can only identify four who were without a doubt "too aggressive." One case involves imitating a fire department official, and another involves a technique that cannot be described in a family newspaper. You don't even want to know about the other two. Suffice it to say that you are not at risk of employing these techniques, or even imagining them.

Don't worry about being overly aggressive. Worry about not being aggressive enough. Unless you sit there and hit "redial" over and over again, you're probably erring on the side of timidity. Here's how to tell if you're over the top: they get on the phone and say, "If you call here one more time we're calling the police." Let that be a sign. Anything short of that, and you're all good.

Also, remember that you have 100 leads at all times. If you upset one of them, so what? You've got ninety-nine more ready to turn to next. Obviously if someone says, "Check in with me in a month," then don't call them every day! But definitely don't wait the full thirty days, either. Three and a half weeks, maybe.

Your "Corps of Helpers"

You need to set up a list of contacts that you consider your corps of helpers. **These are people whom you believe will be the first to hear about a pending opening that matches your interests.** They are probably in the right industry, or they are centers of influence. They are people who routinely come across information that would be critical to getting you in front of a hiring authority early in the staffing selection process, before a posting attracts hundreds of other applicants. "Get other eyes and ears looking with you for what you're looking for," says Richard Bolles, author of *What Color Is Your Parachute* (Ten Speed Press, 2010), the bestselling career book of all time.

As you are gathering information, keep your eye out for people to enroll in your corps of helpers. Ask them for permission to enroll them. "Hey, as my search progresses, I'd really appreciate it if I could call on you from time to time for advice. I respect your opinion, and I think you're pretty knowledgeable in this field. I promise not to be a pest. Would that be all right with you?"

You can also set up a system for getting them to listen for leads for you. "Hey, I know you're busy, but you know practically everybody in _____. I wonder if it would be okay if I were to contact you from time to time to see if you've heard about any news that might impact my search, any companies that are hiring, or any news about business expansion, new product launches, anything like that. If that's all right with you, I could send you an email, and if you haven't heard anything you don't even need to respond. I'll know you don't have anything for me if you don't email me back. Would that be okay?"

These queries, worded this way, have a very high acceptance rate. Then, tickle them on the schedule. Never miss. Never fade away. Some people will not share good leads with you until they see you're serious. If they see you contact them three or four times, right on time, then suddenly they offer up some connections or ideas or advice. They're waiting to see if you're pursuing an idea du jour. Once they see your interest and commitment are not flitting, they decide to help. Anticipate this.

The Railroad Track Letter

There's even a way to get people to become part of your corps of helpers without even speaking to them once. This email is called a Railroad Track Letter, that is, you're enlisting them to keep their ears on the railroad track for news that will be important to your job search.

This is particularly useful for those people who ignore your repeated attempts to connect. After sending this special letter, put the contact person on your calendar for every ten days, and remind them in those tickle emails, "Bart, this is Jan Smith, contacting you again to see if you've heard about anyone thinking about hiring a copywriter. If you've heard something, drop me an email and, as before, if you haven't heard anything, feel free to just disregard this message. I'll be in touch again in ten days. Thanks so much." Then tickle them religiously, every ten days, until you have a solid job offer.

Here's a sample email to set this up:

Dear Bart:

I've been trying to reach you by phone for a week or two now, and we just haven't been able to connect. What I want to talk to you about is this: You're very knowledgeable in the field. You know a lot of people and a lot of people know you. I've refined my job search to a very specific type of opportunity, and I want to know if you'll keep your ears open on my behalf about that opportunity.

Here's what I'm going to propose: If you've heard something that I might benefit from knowing, please take a moment and take or return my contact. But, if you haven't heard anything that will be useful to me, please feel free to not return the contact. That way, I won't be uncomfortable dropping you a message every ten days or so, as my search continues, and I'm hoping that you will agree that this is a minimally invasive way for you to be of potential benefit to two parties, both me and someone out there who is going to want what I bring to the table.

Here's the type of opportunity I'm after _____. [**Be very specific**, e.g., "I want to be a public affairs assistant for a public agency, a governmental or legislative agency, or a corporation in some way active on behalf of education or the public welfare. I'm willing to relocate anywhere, including internationally, to get such a position." This is just an example; write your version to match your interests.]

So, as you go about your normal business, if you hear about anyone considering a staffing change in these areas, give me a "heads-up" and I'll take it from there.

If this is okay, then just keep me in mind. If this is not okay, just reply by email or get on the phone anytime and tell me it's not working out for you.

And of course, if there is anything I can help you with, now or in the future, please don't hesitate to ask.

My greatest appreciation,
I Wanna Job

Champions and Sponsored Mailings

Champions are a special subset of your corps of helpers. You may have an old boss, client, colleague, or cousin who thinks you are special. Champions think you are a genius, or an outstanding performer, or just an all around swell person to work with and know. In short, they love you. In some cases they will be that zenith of a networking resource, someone with a ton of both information *and* power. They may be willing to do much more than a regular contact to ensure your success. Not everyone has any champions, but think carefully if you have one or more.

A champion may be willing to hand you her entire contact list. She almost always volunteers to be a reference. A champion may also be willing to put her name on a sponsored mailing for you. A sponsored mailing is a special category of networking mail. It's when a person asks everyone in her network to afford the same courtesy to you that she would afford to the sponsor herself. Properly done, they are not broadcast blasts "to whom it may concern," but one-to-one missives to all of a person's key contacts. This is the best form of second-tier networking.

Here's an example:

Dear Verna—

I want to alert you to the fact that a former subordinate of mine is on the market, and it could be an opportunity for your advertising agency. She's a research analyst I worked with at Watkins, Linder, Edwards and Shaw. She supported my account team, and I worked with her for over a year on the Mega Brands account. She's one of those rare quant people who understands creative and account services, as well. Certainly one of the very best I've ever worked with, a top 5% employee. She is a careful researcher, excellent at all types of quantitative reasoning, and she can design methodologies as needed. Very, very bright. If you anticipate any adjustments in your quant staffing, please take a look at what she has to offer. We'd be hiring her here at our agency, but we simply do not have a spot for her. I've attached her resume, in case you have a chance to look at it. Let me know if you have any questions, if you want any further information, or if you have any ideas that I should relay to her.

Sincerely,
Parnell A. Campden, account executive, Olveni Advertising

A letter from a champion cuts through the clutter and background noise of the job market. It makes people *who have no search in play and who have not yet posted any opening* ask themselves if they possibly could have a need for your services anytime in the near future.

Also, when you have a champion that is a mutual acquaintance of someone who is considering you for a known opening, a **vouch letter** can be offered up *before* the reference-checking stage. That would look like this:

TO: John Vizlin
SUBJECT: Serena Martenson

John, I sent you an email through LinkedIn (never tried it before) and have no idea if it made it to you. So pardon me if this is redundant. I heard you interviewed Serena for your general counsel position. Having worked with her for seven years, I think very highly of her. If you think she is a serious candidate for the position, I can give you insight into her skills and would be happy to do so. Suffice it to say she is smart, dedicated, tireless, and obviously well schooled in all aspects of the entertainment industry. She's very comfortable and respected within the studio world, and a first-rate and tenacious lawyer. Above all, she is loyal and will have your back always. Hope all is well at the agency. I can tell you that the frequency with which my wife and I patronize your clients' movies should entitle us to at least some free popcorn for a month. Hope to cross paths soon,

Dwight

Dwight Eisenstat | President | Talent Management Council | 900 F Street, NW | Suite 910 | Washington, DC 20004 | 202.555.7984 | DougE@TalentManagementCouncil.org

One warning I have about asking champions for help is the same one I gave you about contacting actual hiring authorities: you'd better be sure about what you want. If you pull the trigger on a sponsored mailing, you can't go back to that champion and say, "Hey, sure appreciate what you did for me on the entertainment law thing, but now I want to be an account executive in PR. Would you mind sending a new mailing to everyone you know about this new idea I have this week?" You see how that's a no go, of course. People who abuse their champions soon find they don't have any.

Mean what you say. Be clear about what you want. Someone who sends a sponsored mailing or inserts himself into hiring decisions on your behalf is doing you a huge, huge favor. You want to honor that asset carefully.

A Problem with Some Executives

One problem with some executive job seekers is that they tend to want to network only with other executives. I know from experience that most executives do not want to participate in outplacement programming with their own rank-and-file employees. They want their own, separate training programs, or they're not happy. If that's you, that's okay. But if you want to do all your networking in a segregated fashion, executive-to-executive only, you will miss a lot of information.

Connecting across lines of generation, class, and power is a skill everyone should develop. The value of information is independent of the source of that information. An executive who refuses to talk to "lower-level" people is just prolonging her job search.

The Most Wrong Way to Do It

When you're in a job search, you're in a marketing campaign. Don't hide this from anybody. Everyone you know should know that you're in the job market, and what type of job you're after. The key to comfort in this process is to make it abundantly clear to all your contacts that you don't expect them to offer you a job.

Two years ago I got a call from a distraught wife of an executive, who was worried about her husband. He was becoming one of the long-term unemployed. She was a highly paid attorney, and they had been careful with their money, so they weren't about to be kicked out in the street. She wasn't really worried about the loss of income. She was worried about her husband as a person. He had been a well-regarded executive. He had been confident, one of those people who embraced life and all it had to offer. Now he was withdrawn, increasingly distant, and had "lost his way," according to her.

Then she told me that he was hiding the fact that he was unemployed. He was telling his friends, "I'm working on some projects that I can't really talk about at this stage. If they work out, I'll tell you all about it." Anyone hearing that would assume he was working on a startup, and certainly not on the job market. In fact, he was presenting to the world that he didn't need any help of any kind. Of course this was all a ruse, and the total opposite of his actual situation!

She bought him some coaching as a gift, and I discovered his deception was even worse than she had described. He actually had a locker down at his country club that was next to a CEO in his same field, *and he had not even mentioned to this guy that he was in the job market.* He was applying for posted openings on the Internet, collecting polite acknowledgements and an occasional ding letter. That was it. His job search was dead. He hadn't had an interview with a hiring authority *in over a year.* And every week he played golf with guys who could have hired him, and they didn't know anything about it.

We role-played his "I'm on the market" speech over and over until he thought he could make his pitch down at the country club. He came out of the closet as a job seeker. He told me he felt liberated, energized. His mood improved. He rededicated himself to finding a job. He built a networking map of everyone he'd ever worked with, and began to contact them systematically.

None of his golf buddies hired him, but all of them had tips and referrals for him. One of those tips led to a job with a startup, in his field and at his salary target. Ironically, he ended up in a startup after all, just as he had been implying for a year. But he never, never, ever would have gotten that job the way he was looking for work before.

8

DUST off YOUR YOUR NETWORK

See a Job Search on the Horizon?

Before you go out and contact everyone you know, ask yourself if you first need to dust off your network. "You have to make friends before you need friends," is an old saying. Do you have lots of acquaintances and friends of friends whom you have not contacted in years? Have you ignored emails from distant connections because you were "too busy" with your own work? You may need to dust off your network before you start asking for job-search assistance. If you're not in an emergency situation, not in the middle of an active and urgent job search, then you might want to spend considerable energy on this. If you think you might find yourself on the job market in the next six months, you should have the foresight to start by dusting off your network.

First, build a list of people who could be particularly useful in your search, and find a reason to contact each and every one of them *before* you ask for job assistance. Old employers, old colleagues, old faculty members, all of them would love to hear from you for some collegial, social reason before you ask for career help. Here are some ideas.

Raise your online profile. First, raise your profile on LinkedIn, Facebook, or any industry news feeds (with comment feature) to which you subscribe. Make comments on blogs and after news posts. For example, most of the query postings I see on social net sites are easy to answer. The poster is either a newbie, who doesn't know something that most people in a profession do know or, often, they're a bit lazy and are asking something that even they could find out by a little searching. The first thing you need to do to raise your profile as a knowledgeable person is to work up quick, thoughtful, and useful responses to these queries. You don't want to be caught doing this, but . . . you can even salt a few soft-balls by having a friend or two ask questions that you have expert answers to. Then, when you hit your social network with a query, people will view you as one of the good guys, one of the contributors, and they'll be much more inclined to put out some effort on your behalf.

You can practice networking, connecting, interviewing, and presenting yourself on Meetup.com and Eventbrite.com. These enable thought leaders and consultants to show off their knowledge and gather communities of practice. These media allow you to organize real-world and virtual events on a daily basis. At a Meetup event it's easy to talk shop and learn from others. You're able to accomplish three missions: Hone your interview skills by discussing what you do best. Connect with people in your field or industry and get industry insider news and tips. And learn about different industry trends so you can talk about them intelligently in later interviews.

Commenting on blogs or answering listserv queries is often as easy as looking at books on your bookshelf for a reference or two, or going to amazon.com or barnesandnoble.com and finding some recent releases from a reputable publisher, or just running a search and digging through some Web pages to build some good links to mention in your response. It's easy for someone who has expertise in his field to come off as thoughtful and knowledgeable with a few minutes' preparation.

Get people to recommend you on LinkedIn. Savvy HR managers will not be overly influenced by gushing recommendations on LinkedIn, but it does show that you at least have friends who think highly of you. If you can get direct bosses to recommend you, that will be noted. Every time you post a recommendation, all your contacts are notified of the update.

Also, when you update your own profile in any way on LinkedIn and other social networks, all your contacts get a notification that you have done so. This, alone, puts your name in their brains. Finally, write some articles, start a blog of your own, comment on other people's blogs, and so on. Again, you should troll for industry-related blogs and add your comments to give you a good online footprint as a knowledgeable and active professional. This gets your name out there.

Use YouTube to present yourself as an expert. Create a how-to vignette that is related to your professional life. Stick to business, and keep it short. Unless you are remarkably funny, your talents with cookie recipes or training dogs will not help you get a job in an office. Three minutes on "Five tips on doing business in the Czech Republic," or four minutes on "How to answer the telephone in a C-level office," or two minutes on "Improving nosocomial outcomes in a long-term care ward" can establish your bona fides as an expert.

This approach has multiple advantages. It helps you prepare for interviews. It gives a positive, professional item if someone does an Internet search on your name. Professionals will stumble across your video, so it has passive advantages. You can also direct people to the video, as an active job-search technique. Finally, it shows that you are able to record and upload a video. Everyone on the market should have some YouTube vignettes that represent his best skills in a quick, tight package. If your interests change, you can pull old versions and post new ones.

Build some recommendation lists on Amazon and Barnes and Noble. If you're an expert in brand development or wedding planning, build some astute and smart lists of recommended readings for www.amazon.com and www.barnesandnoble.com. Use your real name. You'll be identified as an expert by people in your field who are looking at these titles. Also, you can write book reviews for any news feeds or special interest group (SIG) newsletters to which you subscribe.

Forward pertinent articles. Think about your friends and their interests, passions, and avocations. Do you have a friend who loves the Dallas Cowboys? Who collects dolls? Who reads Kellerman novels? Then forward to them articles you happen upon that have to do with their professional or personal interests. "Jessica, I saw this article about your CFO being arrested at La Guardia. Thought you'd want to be the first to know!" "Elizabeth—here's a really cool article I just read about performance-enhancing drugs. Weren't you into that sort of thing?"

It is actually rare to get anything meaningful in the physical mail, so most people are delighted and intrigued to get stuff via snail mail. Cut articles out of newspapers and magazines and send them to those in your network, with a note. Send postcards to people: "I saw this museum show. It's awesome. Thinking of you, Dave Rodriguez." "The beach is great in the winter. Saw that you had 12" of snow! Ouch!—Jordan." Revive the tradition of sending holiday cards in the mail. If it's almost Halloween, that's always good. There are Fourth of July cards now, and even solstice cards. "Hey, Chandra. Merry Christmas! Hope you have a great holiday! Your old pal, Perry." "Hey, Chandra. Happy Hanukkah! I couldn't remember which . . . so I sent you both! Your old pal, Perry."

Raise Your Profile in Your Associations

If you're unemployed or fear being on the job market, you need to kick it up a notch in all your professional associations. Start going to every meeting, obviously, but also join some committees or SIGs. Volunteer for some assignments, like a special event team or a steering committee. Be a mentor. My favorite is to work meetings and events as a registration assistant (you get to meet *everybody*, including VIPs, speakers, and national figures, as well as rank-and-file members), a moderator (you get to meet speakers and panelists, and be seen as a trusted professional), or even an usher (who get roaming privileges to go all over the convention or meeting).

If you have special expertise, find the speaker's committee and pitch a talk for the next regional or national meeting. Or find the journal editor and offer to write an article on the same or similar topics. This is great exposure! It builds your credentials while it raises your profile. If you write an article or do a talk, it gives you a reason to call all the top experts in your field, and you can enroll them in your network. I once worked with an unemployed, partner-level lawyer who was able to give two talks on high-technology law at a meeting, which resulted in several people approaching him with legal work. He ended up abandoning his job search and going into private practice! He found the demand for his topic so great that he didn't need a job to match his old income.

You can do the same in the social, service, or activist organizations to which you belong. If you've not been active lately in your Scrabble, philatelist, or environmental clubs, revive your participation in a noticeable way.

Remember, You Have to Make Friends before You Need Friends

Get more social. Start by reaching back ninety days (or even more) for any emails from distant acquaintances that you blew off. "Hey, my bad! I was just reviewing my emails and noticed that yours got lost in the avalanche. Sorry! So, here's what I think about what you said . . ." You have to make friends before you need friends, so be a good friend. Start going out to coffee and lunch with people inside and outside your organization. Meet those colleagues for drinks even if that's not your kind of thing. Collect business cards from people you meet, however briefly. Get out of your office and out of your building. If you spend a lot of time telecommuting, cut back on that. Go to the office. Go to client sites. Get out and circulate. Show face.

If you do this before you ask people for advice, ideas, leads, and referrals, you're going to get a lot more advice, ideas, leads, and referrals.

9

WHAT TO TALK ABOUT WITH FRIENDS AND STRANGERS

Calls to Action May Vary

In a job search, you'll be exploring some career ideas that you're curious about but not committed to—even as you vigorously apply for other types of jobs that you've already embraced. This is a normal process, but with each contact you will want to be clear about what you're doing, *exploring an idea* or *looking for an opportunity*.

Keep your most immediate goal in mind. Are you just exploring a career idea? Trying to find a way to get your application for a known opening in to one of the employers on your list? Trying to present yourself as a "candidate-in-waiting" for the next opportunity, as it may come available? **The phase you are in and the nature of your contact person determine the appropriate call to action.**

This is extraordinarily important! To explore a career idea you want to find out more information. So your call to action will focus on obtaining that information by any means convenient, be it email, phone call, meeting for coffee, or what have you.

Once you are sure of a goal, focus on hiring authorities and direct referral sources *whether they are hiring or not*. With all hiring authorities you will want to go face to face, and with all direct referral sources you'll want to go face to face or have strong telephone conversations or, if nothing else, a rich exchange of information via email. Your call to action will be to push for a meeting, if possible and practicable, or a phone call if not, or as a last-choice option, an *exchange* of information by email if nothing more can be arranged.

If a hiring authority requests a meeting, or a champion insists you meet with her referrals who are hiring authorities, then of course you follow through and do it. Don't delay or they'll think you're a dud. But when you can control the flow of meetings, follow this principle: delay until you are ready to make a strong case for yourself.

So you see that you will be in different phases on different job ideas. You may be ready to present a strong candidacy for corporate trainer (application phase), while only exploring the idea of being a middle school science teacher (exploration phase). So you'd avoid meeting any school principals (hiring authorities) while you'd actively want to meet with middle school science teachers (people who currently hold the job you want next). Yet, at the same time, you'd be happy to meet hiring authorizes in training and development, as well as meet all levels of corporate trainers (direct referral sources).

In some cases, to meet with hiring authorities that you know you'd like to work for if an opening came up, you may sometimes choose to ask for an **informational interview**, even though you're pretty certain of your interest in the field in general and in that employer in particular. Some people are more amenable to helping people than they are to meeting with prospective employees as a "candidate-in-waiting." However, if you meet with anybody for an informational interview, you had better be sincerely interested in his advice and guidance, or he's going to sense your lack of sincerity and you'll be poisoning the process for everyone else who calls him for help in the future.

Does this all make sense? I hope so, because this really matters.

Informational Interviewing

Informational interviewing is primarily a job-exploration process but, as just mentioned, it can be a tool in the job-search process as well. The explicit goal is for the people you interview to give information to you. However, any job seeker who is still reading this book can guess that there is an implicit goal as well: for you to convey information to them about your skills and potential value, either to them or to someone they may know.

Informational interviews are brief, ten to thirty minutes unless you run into an unexpectedly gracious contact. Some alumni will spend all afternoon with an earnest young alumna or alumnus, for example. Some highly competitive gurus will spend inordinate amounts of time with someone they do not consider a threat, a newbie or someone who obviously doesn't have the skill set to vie for their role, while a potential peer would be slapped down cold. If you have a powerful champion as the source of your referral to the contact, sometimes your contact will give you more time, as well.

Informational interviewing is related to **shadowing.** Shadowing is when you ask to observe a careerist as he goes about his professional day. Shadowing can last an afternoon to a couple of days. (Compare this to the Hercules offer, page 131.) Shadowing is really a process for college and graduate students. It's too big a favor to request for most people who don't have extraordinary connections to the contact (for example, the contact is your aunt's employee).

Your call to action when seeking an informational interview should be to set up face-to-face meetings when you can be in the same location, and telephone interviews when that is not possible. It is not unusual for college students to go on informational interviewing and shadowing junkets. For example, if their college is in a rural locale, and they are interested in bright lights and big cities, they may arrange to be in Manhattan or Chicago for days at a time to go on informational interviews and shadow successful alumni. There is nothing to prevent a job seeker who is not a college student from setting up similar informational meetings in distant cities of interest.

There are tons of great interview books on the market, but almost no guides on how to act at an informational interview. Keep in mind that when you are going to an informational interview, you are entering into an organization's space and using that organization's resources under the auspices of looking for information. It is by their grace that you are there. It is a gift to you. Take this very seriously, and be a good guest.

All the usual rules of etiquette for interviewing apply. You will call and confirm the day before. No matter how difficult the travel logistics, you will arrive a few minutes early at the appointed location. You will look, walk, and talk like a professional. You will have researched the organization and your interviewee before the meeting. You will have questions ready. You will send a prompt thank-you note after the meeting.

You will be interviewing your contact, rather than the other way around. She should be doing most of the talking. You are there to extract information, efficiently, and to express appreciation for the opportunity to do so.

Here are some standard informational interviewing questions:

"How did you get into this field?" Everybody is an expert in herself, and almost everybody likes to talk about herself, so this is a great icebreaker. Listen to her story.

"What kind of preparation is typical for your position? Is that really required, or just the typical approach?" Listen for the secret handshake, the key background experience that identifies you as qualified to gain entry.

Be skeptical of "requirements" that are mythological. For example, someone may say that you have to have a technical degree in order to do her type of work, and you find out she was an English major.

"What was different from what you expected? What was the biggest surprise when you went into this field? Any myths you want to shatter for me?" Many careers are very different than their television versions. Litigators are rarely in court. Cops never fire their guns. People in the fashion industry work months and months to put something on the runway for a few seconds. So your goal is to find out the "behind the scenes" truth about the field in question. What's it *really* like?

Avoid the question, "Can you describe a typical day?" Anyone in hiring is sick of that question. Nevertheless, you need to find out what people do all day. Learn the nature of the work itself. Find out if there are seasons or deadlines, or if it is more of a steady pace all year-round. Find out if you would be working alone a lot, and if people in this role normally telecommute or if they have to show face at the office every day. Scope out how much travel would be involved. Always ask, "How is success measured?" Watch out for responsibility without authority, a formula for misery. These kinds of work-style questions are important to make sure your preconceptions are accurate.

"Who else does this? What other companies? Who else should I be talking to?" This is probably the most important question series you will ask. You may be chipping away at the tip of the iceberg, and questions like these will reveal the whole structure. This is the line of inquiry that gives you the information to continue in your quest!

"What ensures continued advancement?" You need to know how to excel once you get into this new position. To get promoted, you may need to master certain assignments, such as being successful abroad. You may need to pick up another degree or credential.

"What is the typical career path out of this position or field? What does this prepare you for next? For example, what's next for you?" These questions have to do with career pathing. In some industries, to get to the top you must rotate through assignments, while in others you can just keep getting promoted within the functional area you already inhabit. For example, to make hotel general manager, you have to rotate. An ambitious person will spend some time in sales, rooms division (front desk), food and beverage, and housekeeping. If you get hung up in any area, you're not headed for general manager. Anyone in a hotel can tell you this. Career paths really matter, and the more ambitious you are the more they matter. In traditional industry, some departments can lead to the top (finance and operations), while others usually lead only to department head (human resources). You can use informational interviews to map out your long-view plan.

"What advice do you have for someone like me?" A nice, open-ended query like this should be included in any informational interview. People who have agreed to meet with you have their own agenda. They have their own set of points they want to convey to you. So give them a chance to lay it out. Asking for advice is a great way to learn. You'll get conflicting advice. You'll get discouragement from some connections, and an enthusiastic endorsement of your plans from others. You'll even get conflicting advice from the same person! All of this is normal. But watch for patterns! If everybody says you'll have to move to L.A. to break into the movie business, then either start packing or modify your goal.

Finally, if you are comfortable with your contact, and particularly if you *don't* think you're ever going to work there, you might have a question or two about salary or income potential. Be careful! If you ask about salary, don't ask about her salary or salaries at her company. Ask, "What could a person expect to make in a position like this?" Or, "What would be a typical salary industry-wide for a position like this?" Then subtract 10 to 40 percent. Humans tend to exaggerate incomes, even other people's incomes.

You might create a cheat sheet of questions you want to work into the conversation, but let the conversation flow. It's probably best not to act like a cop or a reporter for an ambush news show. Don't go straight down your list of questions, but at some point you might glance at your notes to make sure you don't miss anything important.

When you go into an information interview, you'll want to travel light. No big backpack, and briefcases are so 1989. If you come in dragging a small suitcase, everyone will think you're selling mini fridges or something. My recommendation is to go with the padfolio. That's a small leather or vinyl folder just large enough to cover a pad of writing paper, and usually with pockets into which you can slip some resumes and a few copies of your business card.

You will be expected to have a resume and a business card. Give everyone in the world your business card, but don't offer the resume unless it is requested. The best job-seeker cards have your name and contact information and a pretty specific hint of what kind of employment the seeker is after. On the following page are two examples, one for a young person with a new graduate degree, and another for someone a little deeper into his career.

Ruby Jewel

M.P.A., Concentration in Public Finance and Program Assessment
University of Wisconsin

Areas of Knowledge:
- Public Finance
- Program Auditing & Assessment
- IT and Information Systems Design
- Fluent in Spanish (read, write, translate)

rubyjewel@aol.com   39 Elm Street
(765) 555-1423   West Lafayette, IN 47907

Dustin Jossophan

European Sales Representative, Financial Software

Offering:
- English, French, German (fluent)
- Flemish, Swedish, Finnish (proficient)
- Knowledge of Global Accounting Standards (IASB)
- Knowledge of U.S. FASB and GAAP
- M.Sc., LSE; A.B. Princeton

dustinjoss@euro.com   London and New York
                         U.S.A. phone (24/7) 212-555-7549

If it makes you nervous to commit to a career direction, "Account Executive in Advertising," then make two cards, one where you are obviously seeking that specific goal, and another that just has contact information. That way, when you run into an exciting opportunity to supervise a foreign exchange program for a school system, you don't have to hand them your "advertising" card.

You can get free business cards by running a search on "free business cards." Or you can get special business card paper at any office supply and print your own. Don't leave home without them.

Converting an Informational Interview into an Application Interview

Whenever you are conducting informational interviews, you will stumble across promising openings for internships, consulting contracts, temporary assignments, and permanent positions. If you want to apply for one of these opportunities, you must apply for a change in status. In other words, you will need to get permission to convert from being an information seeker to being an applicant for an opening.

As a good informational interviewer, you are a polite novice seeking access to insider information. As an applicant, you are a confident provider of needed skills, seeking an appropriate fit or match. These are very different conditions, that is, they are very different presentations of self. So you have to convert your status as a novice information seeker into a competent potential contributor. Also, managers who grant access to you on the basis of providing information are doing you a favor. They may resent it greatly if you suddenly start applying for an open position. This is not graceful. What you must do is *apply for permission to apply,* that is, ask for permission to apply for one of the opportunities that became known in the conversation.

Apply for a change in status by saying this: **"That sounds like a very interesting opportunity. How would I go about formally applying for that position?"** By saying something like this, you are acknowledging that you are not at that point a candidate for anything but information. You are asking them for their advice about whether you can or should apply for the opening, and how to proceed if they grant you permission.

Then, follow their instructions precisely. The very best response you can get is something like this: "Well, I know the woman who's doing the hiring for that position. You wait right here and I'll just drop your resume on her desk right now, and see if she can meet with you today." That won't happen very often, but that is the most desired outcome.

More often you'll hear some version of: "Just apply online." To which you should promptly say, "Great. I'll do that. May I mention your name as a referral?"

I've analyzed employment websites and how they sort applicants. In almost all of them there is a huge bias in favor of candidates referred by current employees. Employee referrals go right to the top of the queue, often even if they don't match the skills or experience requirements for the posted opening! You always want permission to be referred.

Informational Interviewing Is a Privilege

Please, please do not mess up informational interviewing! If candidates who do not genuinely want information go out there and abuse this technique as a subterfuge to meet with hiring authorities, then this process will be ruined for everybody. Informational interviewing is absolutely critical for young people who are just learning about the world of work, who are exploring where they might fit in best, and for career changers, who are trying to discover how their skills and aptitudes might be valued in a new industry or field. *Use informational interviewing only when you are going to embrace the information you discover.* Any thinly veiled applications disguised as informational interviews will anger and disappoint your contacts.

Be on time, go in and get your information quickly, be professional, send a prompt thank-you card, and follow the advice you receive. That's the right way to do it. If you feel any warmth, enroll them in your corps of helpers.

By the way, informational interviewing is a lifetime skill. I teach C-level executives how to do it. There is never a time when you are past the point where you cannot benefit from getting advice from people you would like to emulate. Repeat until retired.

Let's Do Lunch

In his instant classic networking guide, *Never Eat Alone: And Other Secrets to Success, One Relationship at a Time* (Broadway Business, 2005), author Keith Ferrazzi does a masterful job of positioning meals as unique networking opportunities. Ferrazzi was the youngest partner in Deloitte Consulting's history and founder of the consulting company Ferrazzi Greenlight. He also has a companion blog for the book, nevereatalone.typepad.com.

For our purposes, here's the point: people who would never let you into their offices or their lives will gladly meet you for lunch, especially if you're buying and most especially if you're bringing along a mutual acquaintance.

I recognize that lunch is expensive, and most job seekers need to watch their nickels and dimes. On the other hand, lunch is a magic "open sesame" to hiring authorities and direct referral sources. Under the lightest of pretexts, I will meet someone for lunch and let them ask me a thousand questions. The weird thing is that my hourly rate right now is $275, but buy me a $30 lunch and I give it up for free. I am a complete sucker for this line: "I'd love to ask you some questions and get your advice. I'd be happy to take you out to lunch this week, if you have any time at all. I'll pick up the tab and have you back in the office right on time."

There's nothing unusual about me. There is a switch in people's brains that tells them that this is a great deal. Make it absolutely clear that you'll be picking up the tab, and voilà, you've got a meeting.

If you have a mutual acquaintance, that makes the whole thing seem safer. You can't be a bore if our mutual acquaintance is willing to spend her lunch with us, too.

If you're trying to avoid picking up too many tabs, you can also meet all your friends and acquaintances "in the industry" for lunch meetings. These types of quick, business lunches are almost always Dutch, and you have to eat anyway. I want you out and about for the duration of your job search, so get dressed up, head downtown, and start meeting people for lunch. Just connecting up for lunch has less power over your contacts than buying them lunch (for example, they may cancel on you at the last moment), but it's a great way to see and be seen.

Make a list of people you want to share a lunch or power breakfast with, then get busy inviting them out to meet you, or yourself out to meet them. If you want a quick guide on collecting people, I recommend my professional acquaintance Diane Darling's *Networking for Career Success: 24 Lessons for Getting to Know the Right People* (McGraw Hill, 2005).

10

ENGAGING POSSIBLE EMPLOYERS

The Candidate-in-Waiting Meeting

If you're trying to meet with hiring authorities who are not at that moment hiring, you need a rationale for why they should spend time with you. One of the valid rationales is that you are interested in their advice and more information about careers and career paths. This is informational interviewing, and we just covered that process. Another one of the better rationales is the idea that they are doing a favor for a mutual acquaintance, especially a high-status person who is asking for the connection on your behalf. Those are both perfectly valid reasons for people to give up some minutes in their day.

However, a third rationale is also powerful: you would like to be considered a **candidate-in-waiting**, in case something opens up later in their organization. Smart managers know that at any moment key staff members could disappear from their team. A critical performer can turn disloyal, take a job somewhere else, retire, have a heart attack, or develop a crippling addiction to pain relievers and be shipped off to months of rehab. Staffing is a critical management skill. Being able to attract, develop, and motivate strong contributors is a highly valued skill. It leads to recognition and promotions. So, savvy managers are constantly scanning the horizons for talent.

In fact, there is a coming war for talent. In HR circles there was, before the last recession, a wave of fear about the demographic trough following the baby boomers. The generation after the boomers is 15 percent smaller than the boomer wave. Take an historical average of about 3 percent economic growth and combine it with a 15 percent demographic contraction, and you have an 18 percent shortage of qualified managers! This really is a crisis in development. It's happening in slow motion and the Great Recession has been a speed bump in the process—but it is absolutely already underway. Baby boomers are starting to exit stage right, and there is a shortage of *highly skilled managers* to take their place.

(We will continue to have a surplus of uneducated, incompetent, and underperforming workers.)

Organizations use business crises to weed their gardens. They quite intentionally ditch undesirable staff. Everybody knows that. But they also have to cut good people who are in bad positions, the good people who are unlucky enough to be in divisions, branches, and business lines that are not sustainable in bad times.

Smart managers can see down the road to their staffing needs as circumstances evolve. Although the job market in your field today where you are living may not indicate this, there is an historic shift of power going on right now, away from employers and toward high-skill workers. If you are a high-skill worker, hiring authorities may be willing to talk to you anytime, to keep you in the queue in case an opening appears down the road.

Here's a sample script for presenting this rationale: "I understand that you're not hiring right now. I'd like to meet with you briefly, anyway, to show you what I've done and kick around ideas about how I might be of value to you. That way, when an opening comes up later, you'll think of me first. I think my track record will be of interest to you, and a few minutes now could save you a lot of trouble if you need to make a sudden staffing adjustment. I'll be in and out of your office in fifteen minutes, and we'll both know if there is any chemistry for the future."

This rationale works, and the real beauty to it is that it works best at the best places, that is, places where the managers are the smartest and most prescient. Smart, fast-growing companies are always looking for good talent. Kevin P. Ryan, CEO of AlleyCorp in New York City, says he is always on the prowl for good people: "I have an understanding with certain search firms that if you find someone great, don't wait until there's a job opening—send him to me."

Why don't you take a few minutes and write your own version of this rationale now? Read it aloud several times, so it will come naturally to you the next time a key contact says, "We're not hiring."

"Possible Employers" and the Tickle List

Your calls and meetings should generate an exponentially increasing amount of follow-up for you, as each connection leads you to ideas, leads, and referrals that must then be explored. Your efforts should lead you to discover some known openings (which we'll explore more fully in the next chapter). They should also lead you to identify a large volume of organizations that could hire you if they were in need of additional staffing. As you go along with your search, you should be able to build a list of "possible employers," places where you think you would be happy to be employed. Of course you will throw out some potential employers because you discover they have a toxic atmosphere or are unattractive for other reasons. That leaves an increasingly growing list of workplaces where you think you could fit in.

You need to stay in touch with people at those organizations. If you use the railroad track technique or ask permission to enroll them in your corps of helpers, then you can just naturally check in with them every couple of weeks or so. My suggestion is that when you can, when it is appropriate, mix in some social connections with your job-search tickles.

Learn to write emails that do not require a response! This puts you inside their brains with low cost for either one of you. "Hey, saw this and thought you'd find it interesting," does not require a response. "Congratulations on your divorce, and good luck with your new marriage! Best wishes," does not require a response. Get in the habit of reading your missives one last time before hitting "send." If you're just massaging your network, you'll want a lot of these emails to not require a return comment, even at the emoticon level.

Again, to do this systematically, you'll need to know when you last contacted someone, and when you would like to find a reason to contact her again. This will vary by contact, but make it intentional, not accidental.

The Contingent World and the Hercules Offer

You will run into posted openings as you network, opportunities for full-time, permanent, career-track positions with full benefits. Some of these openings will be in the formation stage, which is ideal, and others will already be announced and receiving hundreds of applications. Of course you should pursue *every single one* of these.

You may also run into all kinds of other opportunities as you are connecting with a lot of people. You may get invitations to start businesses, invitations to purchase products and services you don't need or want, invitations to go on dates (even if you are obviously married), and so on. That's just part of the process; don't let it bother you.

There is, however, another type of opportunity that you want to be constantly on the watch for, and that is the chance to join an organization on a contingent basis by picking up a consulting assignment or some other kind of "try-out" project. Many jobs do not start out as full-time, permanent, career-track positions with full benefits. Many jobs start out as contingent opportunities, that is, **part-time, temporary, or contract assignments.**

This includes the classical internship for college students and recent grads, but it increasingly includes all types of jobs at all levels. I recently worked with a CFO who was first hired on an interim basis, and went on to become the official CFO after taking the company through a contentious SEC filing.

Contingent jobs are one path to permanent, full-time employment and—even when that's not the case—they keep your skills sharp and provide income while you continue your search.

Hiring authorities might be very amenable to hiring you on a contingent basis even if they had not been considering hiring anyone in such a role. Remember, all an employer has to believe in order to hire you is (a) he likes you, and (b) you'll be useful to have around, that you'll create more value for the organization than the cost of employing you.

Be agreeable when a hiring authority says, "Well, we could use some help on a project, but I'm not sure we have any permanent openings that would match your skill set." Perk up! That's a line of conversation to pursue. You may be able to secure a consulting engagement, while continuing to present yourself as a potential hire to the employer.

One variant on this is the **Hercules offer.** That's when you offer to perform some task for the hiring authority, to gain her grace and consideration for deeper engagement. Maybe she mentions being overworked and unable to complete some special project. Or maybe you see some study or investigation you could do for her that would be of benefit for her, while showcasing your skills and abilities.

As one example: I once hired someone on the spot who came to her first interview with a market analysis of my company and all similar companies in San Francisco. She had called all of my competitors, and developed a menu of their services and pricing. She prepared positioning and psychographic profiles for each business, showing my firm at the top in terms of our services, mission, and level and type of client we were targeting. It was flattery in part, of course, but it was also highly effective. No doubt she had already done this to make sure she was interested in joining my firm at all. It was little trouble for her to prepare it as a report.

The Hercules offer is often an unpaid performance, just short of consulting and with no deeper obligation for either party.

If you really like an organization, try to think up a Hercules offer, something you can offer that would be of great interest and no cost to them, and little cost to you. This is a deceptively simple technique that can open up a relationship that is on the verge.

11

OBJECTIONS AND GATE-KEEPERS

Overcoming Objections

I discovered from my own research into sales theory and sales training that objections are a fascinating linguistic phenomenon. Objections are a part of conversation, and conversation is like a volley in tennis. They say something, then you say something. It doesn't matter really what you say when it is your turn to speak, as long as you keep the conversation going. Therefore, if you ever let an objection terminate a conversation, you made the choice to terminate it, not your partner in the conversation.

If they say, "We're not hiring," and you say, "Gosh, sorry to bother you," then *you* and *you alone* abandoned that conversation.

Objections are neither literal nor logical. The meaning behind an objection may be quite different from the words that are used to convey that meaning. "I don't really know anything that would be of use to you" may mean "I'd love to help you, but I'm sitting here hoping that you don't ask me for a job, because I like you and I don't want to be put into the uncomfortable position of saying 'no' to you. Besides, the whole idea of unemployment scares me, and if you sound desperate it might just totally creep me out." You can overcome this objection in advance, by making it clear that you are not asking them for a job, and by being enthusiastic about your search and the world of possibility out there.

Thus, you don't have to overcome the objection *logically* in order to dismiss it. In fact, a very advanced technique is simply to agree with the objection. "I'm too busy to meet with you" is completely disarmed when you say, "Yeah, I heard you guys were really successful right now. That's great." Suddenly, it's the other person's turn to speak, and the conversation continues.

There may be a pause, and you may want to fill that pause, but don't. It's the other person's turn, and I assure you he'll jump in there soon enough. He'll jump in with something like "Well, how could I assist you? I'm underwater with work, so a face-to-face is out, but what else could I do that might help you out?" That's what you want to happen.

In fact, **objections appear right before someone decides to help you.** In sales theory, the sale only begins with the objections. If someone is really blowing you off, she just says, "Yes, yes. I'll keep you mind. Thanks for calling. Yep. Okay. Goodbye." That's someone who is not going to help you at all. If she says "Your experience is all in retail, and we're wholesale here," then that's someone who is about to help you. Remember, you don't have to overcome the logic of the objection. It's fine if you have a quip about how your retail experiences are transferrable, but really, that's not the point. Don't worry about the content of objections at all; just keep the conversation going until you get to advice, ideas, leads, and referrals. When you hear an objection, you should cheer because you're interacting with someone who is paying attention to your situation.

Sales professionals are trained to listen for objections, and they're also trained to work into objections two and five levels deep. In a sale, the first objections are usually trivial and obvious, but the fifth or sixth or so are real. So, the fact that your background is in retail is no big deal, but if deep into a meeting about referring you to the boss your friend says you dress funny, then that's a problem that has to be resolved. That's a real objection to advancing you.

Objections are a "buy" signal. Watch for them and enjoy your ability to go through, over, or around them.

As you conduct your job search, you will run into the same four objections over and over again.

1. We're not hiring.

2. I'm too busy.

3. Send me your resume.

4. Just apply online.

Here are some responses to these common objections:

GETTING AROUND THE FOUR MOST COMMON OBJECTIONS

"We're not hiring."

- That's okay. I'm not applying for a job with you anyway. I am just interested in your advice.

- That's okay. I'm not in any hurry. I just wanted you to know what I have to offer in case something opens up later.

- That's okay. I just wanted to know if you would take a look at my resume and give me any advice, ideas, leads, or referrals that come to mind.

- That's okay. Perhaps you can think of someone else who might be interested right now in what I have to offer. Your referral could be appreciated by both of us.

"I'm too busy."

- This'll only take a moment.

- Yeah. I heard you guys were pretty successful right now.

- I'd be happy to meet you early, late, during lunch, even after work. What's best for you?

- What's a better time for me to connect?

"Send me your resume, and I'll take a look at it."

- Well let me tell you what's on it.

- I'm not really applying for a position with you but, sure, I'd like it if you'd look at it and give me any feedback that you think would help. Thanks.

- What's your email? I'll email it to you while we are speaking.

- I'll bring it to the meeting. What's a good time for you?

"I'm not the person you should be talking to." Or **"Just apply online."**

- But I'm not applying for a job. I got your name from _____. She said you were quite knowledgeable about this field. I just want to know if you would have a moment to share with me any advice, ideas, leads, and referrals.

- Actually, I'm going to be applying through "official" channels, as well, but I wondered if you could give me a little inside information.

- Who should I be talking to about this? I appreciate the referral. May I mention your name?

- Great! What's the best way for me to proceed?

Getting Around Gatekeepers

Gatekeepers stand between you and your networking contact, direct referral source, or hiring authority. Electronic gatekeepers are the most common type, now, so you'll have to get past email filters and telephone answering devices, all intended to keep you out. Occasionally you'll run into a live human being whose job it is to keep you from appearing in the mind of the decision maker. He'll block your calls, fail to give your messages as intended, and otherwise act like you're an annoying intrusion. Of course you are the very best employee they have not yet hired, so you should not take any of this personally. It's not that they don't love you; they just don't know you yet.

Email is the first step. Remember that people have multiple email addresses and multiple settings for screens and filters. Anyone whose name appears on an organization's website, or who appears publicly for an organization as a corporate officer, spokesperson, or representative, is very likely to have a public email with high screens that she checks seldom, and a different day-to-day email that she lives by. Anytime someone's email becomes public on the Internet, he will be buried in spam. That means high filters and sometimes only occasionally wading through the junk to see if anything important came by.

If an email query is worth sending once, it's worth sending correctly. Always use the three-shot method on any known emails. (1) Email. (2) Wait three days; send the same email again. (3) Wait four days; send the same email with a new top on it, "Dr. Wilson, I'm not sure I have an accurate email address for you. What follows is what I've been trying to find out last week and this. I'd be truly grateful if you'd have even a moment to respond." Then put the original email below that.

Repeat this process for every email you can find or guess for a contact, then check LinkedIn and Plaxo to query him. Finally, go to Facebook or MySpace and poke him. Remember, younger people don't use email as much as the rest of us. If your contact is a currently enrolled college student, I'd be tempted just to jump to Facebook early on. If you want to learn how to find people online, read articles by David Sarokin at eHow.com (and elsewhere). He's made a hobby out of exploring and sharing techniques that work.

Guessing emails is easier than you think. Look at the emails you can find on an organization's website. If they are structured first initial, last name, then so will be your contact in most cases. Likewise if they are structured first name, underscore, last name, or first initial plus first four letters of last name, and so on. Anyone who ever hacked in high school knows that you can guess emails and passwords if you know someone's full name, nicknames, date of birth, spouse's name, pets, kids, and so on. It's a lot easier than getting a corporation to hand over someone's email address, frankly. Don't start hacking passwords, but do work at guessing email addresses.

It's laborious, but the best way to overcome filters and screens is to send your email directly to one person. From you, to her. No copies and no mailing list. Also, don't email from a known spamming domain, which unfortunately includes many of the most popular free email providers. Want to know the safest email domains? Major colleges and universities. They have vigorous and diligent IT officers, and they rank really high on security algorithms used by major search engines and spam filters. Your alumni email account, especially if you went to Stanford or Berkeley or Princeton, may be a great choice for the duration of your job search.

While we're on this topic, what does your email say about you? If your email is hotfoxy69@hotmail.com or devilboy666@hades.org, you're not in the professional job market. A recruiter recently told me about an email he got from a graduate student. She was a good prospect. He liked her query, and had written a response encouraging her to apply, when he noticed her email was butterfly24@university.com. He had his finger in the air, ready to hit "send," when he said to himself, "Butterfly24. Hhmmn. We're really not a butterfly kind of place." He opted for "delete."

Automated telephone screens. Telephone answering systems have made calling people much easier because you don't have to justify yourself to a receptionist or secretary. The key is to get someone's extension, which is usually on their business card, if you have one of those. Or the person who gave you the lead may give you their extension number if you explicitly ask for it. Alternately, somewhere in the phone tree you can usually find a directory, where by spelling the person's last name on the number keys or dividing the Zodiac by pi, you will eventually be rewarded with someone's extension number.

Then you can call them directly. Here's one really important thing to remember: they know who you are. Your number and often your name will show up on their incoming call LED. Many call systems block all callers who conceal their own phone number, so that's not going to work out for you on average. The only ramification to the fact that they know who you are is that you cannot call them over and over on the same day. A young person who attended one of my workshops misinterpreted something I said, and just sat down and called a contact over and over and over and over and over. She got a cup of coffee or a Mountain Dew, sat down at her desk, and just started hitting redial. Don't do that.

The etiquette for business telephone calls is really clear. You can call people once in the morning, and once in the late afternoon, *forever.* **You should leave only one message per day.** If they don't take the call or call you back, you are perfectly within your rights to keep calling. Now you would not want to do this with a high-value contact—say, a member of the board of a company you would like to work for. That's overkill. But if it is that friend of an ex-husband's tennis buddy's dog walker's accountant, then you can go all out.

Business etiquette is distinctly different from social etiquette. In social etiquette, calling someone over and over is called stalking. In business it's called being serious. If you are nice and polite, and you call people every day and leave nice and polite messages, they learn three things about you: you're nice, you're polite, and you're persistent. Those are positive attributes in a new hire, or in a colleague or acquaintance.

If you're leaving a message, don't ask them to call you back! They won't anyway, and they'll feel guilty about it. Here's a script for leaving a message:

Script for voicemail: "Hello. This is Donald Asher. I'm sorry to have missed you. I was referred to you by our mutual acquaintance, Emily Matson. My number is 415-543-7130, but there's no need to ring me back. I'll be calling again."

Then, of course, you must call again. As many times as it takes.

How Far Is Too Far? How Much Is Just Enough?

You may be thinking that I'm advocating harassment. You may be thinking that this is too aggressive. *It is not.* The very moment people say, "Hey, stop calling me," you stop. But until you hear those words, you are perfectly within the bounds of business etiquette to keep calling them—once in the morning, once in the late afternoon, but only leaving one message, at most, per day.

If you're really shy you could call them every other day. If you're really, really shy you could call them on Mondays and Wednesdays, forever.

This is not illegal, immoral, or unethical. It might become annoying, over time, but it is not out of bounds in any way. So what if you're annoying sometimes? Big deal! That's not a sin. On the other hand, you probably wouldn't want to do this for every contact. This is a tool in your toolbox. It's a skill, a technique that you can deploy, when it will really matter.

If you believe a particular contact has a chance to make a big difference in your search, to be a game changer if you could just connect, then you need to put out some extra effort. It's not her job to contact you. Remember, she may be interested in speaking with you. She may be looking forward to it. But she's busy, she got more than 100 emails today, she got twenty phone calls that have to do with urgent matters, and so you fall by the wayside in the everlasting waterfall of business communications.

Your contact may be sitting there in his office saying, "I wonder when that nice young person from my alma mater is going to call me again. I really want to chat with her. I hope she calls me back. I don't even know where I put her phone number. Oh, well."

Or maybe she's saying to herself, "Gosh, too bad my computer died and I lost all that data. I really wanted to get back to that guy I used to work with. He was a great guy, and he probably thinks I'm blowing him off. If only I hadn't lost that hard drive! I probably should switch systems to cloud computing with 100 percent real-time backup. I hope that guy calls again or emails me so we can connect."

I always ask people in workshops: Think about a really big world problem; how far would you go if you *personally* could solve a really big world problem? Let's address hunger. According to the World Food Programme, over one **billion** people go to bed every night without enough to eat. Wouldn't you make a few extra phone calls to eradicate the problem of hunger in the world? One billion people helped by your effort? You're uncomfortable for a few moments, and one billion people eat.

Sure, you would make those calls. Now let's bring this closer to home. Would you make a few extra phone calls to eradicate hunger in your house?

Take a cold look in the mirror. How far would you go to protect you and yours? Yes, it's true that you won't be calling most people day after day, but once in a while you're going to have a contact that is so high value that you are going to pursue him, steadily, doggedly, repeatedly, for weeks and weeks before you either make the connection or give up on him entirely.

There is no maximum effort, no excessive length, as long as you stay within the clear bounds of business etiquette. At the other end of the spectrum, what's minimum performance? In my mind, you shouldn't reach out to anybody unless you're willing to email her three times using the three-shot system, and you shouldn't call anyone unless you're willing to call several times, and leave at least three polite messages, over a week and a half. That's minimum effort. Less than that, and you don't get the point of this book at all.

Human gatekeepers. Human gatekeepers are those receptionists, secretaries, and coworkers of your targeted contact who screen her telephone calls. They are your nemesis, but you cannot afford to anger or alienate them. Never underestimate the power of support staff! Those of us who study corporate culture know that they are the unseen dark matter of the organizational universe. Trendy initiatives and executive saviors may come and go, but the support staff live on forever. They are the oil or sand that keeps the wheels of commerce going or not. If they like you, you will be immensely benefitted, and if they dislike you, your candidacy will be a non-starter.

Rule #1: Be nice to support staff. They deserve it as human beings, and it's in your self-interest anyway. (Hot tip: send the receptionist a thank-you note after interviews. It will impress him;

he'll show it to the boss, and you'll look thoughtful, kind, and thorough. Do not send flowers or candy or mush cards; they make you look like an idiot.)

Rule #2: Be honest when speaking directly with support staff. Professional secretaries can smell dishonesty and subterfuge better than a snarling dog can smell fear. All day every day they fend off clever sales professionals with years more practice than you.

You need to recognize that your goals are directly at odds with a gatekeeper's goals. He wants to screen you out as just another distraction to the decision maker. A decision maker's time is valuable, and the gatekeeper's job is to protect it. Your goal is to get through the gatekeeper and let the decision maker decide for herself if you are worthy of her time. A decision maker may be delighted to talk with you or meet with you, but she cannot make that determination if your request is screened entirely.

Here are several ways to get around, over, or through gatekeepers:

Avoid being a job seeker, at first. Whenever you can, avoid being a job seeker at the point of first contact. Job seekers are routinely banned from reaching decision makers. So do your best to be anything other than a job seeker. Be a personal friend, obviously, if you are one. Be a seeker of information, a friend of a friend with a quick question, or a pal from the golf club with a query that "will only take a moment." Throughout the process avoid sending anyone emails with a resume attached, because that automatically makes you a job seeker. In fact, never say the word "resume" at all.

If they say, "What is this call regarding?" and you are a personal friend, you can say, "I'm a friend of hers and this is a personal call. She'll recognize my name." This is only a good idea if she will recognize your name, of course. When you can say this truthfully, it has a very high rate of success at getting past gatekeepers' screens. You can help by telling the gatekeeper how you know the contact. "Our kids were in the same karate class," or "We were both going out with Tiger at the same time back in 2009" will give your contact a chance to remember you.

Tricks really backfire for most job seekers. "I'm a friend of a friend, and I'm inviting her to a party," works fabulously at getting through the screen, but then the gatekeeper will find out you are a liar, and the decision maker will be angry at you and the gatekeeper. So, even if you are tempted to use some of these types of gambits, don't.

Ultimately, you cannot avoid being a job seeker, because you are one. But give someone a chance to put the call through before that becomes evident.

Cite a referral, especially a high-status one. All referrals invoke authority. In most cases, the gatekeeper cannot be sure whether the decision maker will want to talk to someone who has been referred. If you can cite a referral with more status than the person you are trying to call, you have an even higher chance of getting through. Being "referred down" has tremendous power.

In workshops I tell people to practice saying, "Dr. Lee from M.I.T. suggested I give her a call." Of course, in the real world this has to be true. Interestingly enough, there are at least ten Dr. Lees at M.I.T., so they can't get to the bottom of the matter while you are on hold. Just kidding.

If they say, "What is this call regarding?" and you are a friend of a friend, you can say, "I'm a friend of her former boss at Watson & Wilson, and I just have a quick question for her. Pete Simpson said I should give her a call. She knows Pete."

You can always say, because it is true, "Donald Asher suggested that I give her a call." Just kidding, again, although a workshop attendee did actually use that technique and it worked just fine. The reason I know the workshop attendee actually did this is that I got a call from someone who knew who I was. She told me all about it and she asked me to cut it out. Nevertheless, just for the record, she did talk to the caller!

All joking aside: always cite your referral. You are borrowing some of her authority and most gatekeepers will go ahead and put you through, so the decision maker can decide for herself whether your query is worthy of her time. Never forget that really important and successful people also like to help people, and really important and successful people may have a soft spot for callers from their alma maters, from their church, or who remind them of themselves at an earlier stage in life, and so on.

Let the decision maker decide whether she will assist you. If you chicken out and never call, or wimp out and fold because some gatekeeper says "boo," you're robbing that decision maker of a chance to decide for herself.

Mention precisely when you will call in an email or letter. Then you can tell the gatekeeper, "She's expecting my call." This is a little slick, but it works. Be ready to answer the follow-up question, "Yes, but what shall I tell her this call is regarding?" Mail any kind of letter, card, or note with lines like these: "I will call you on Tuesday at 10:30 A.M. You can count on me to be prompt. I look forward to our conversation." It doesn't matter if you say what the call is about.

Call at 7:40 A.M., 10:05 A.M., 12:20 P.M., 2:05 P.M., 5:25 P.M. See the pattern? The gatekeeper is not on duty. The meaner the gatekeeper, the more likely he takes his breaks right on time. If you call during a break, you get the relief gatekeeper. The relief gatekeeper resents having to serve in this capacity at all, and so she often puts everybody through out of spite. Rarely is she dedicated to protecting decision makers. Her heart is just not in it. "Oh, you want Cyndi Parson? I'll put you right through. Please hold." Boom. You're in.

Dial around. The contact's phone number is 555-1200. That gatekeeper has been carefully screening you out. So you dial 555-1201, 555-1202, 555-1203, etc. Sooner or later somebody answers the phone with something like, "Engineering." You say, "Engineering. Gosh. I don't need engineering. I'm trying to reach Cyndi Parson. Can you put me through or tell me her direct extension. Thanks." (Notice that there is no lie in that statement.)

Call once a day until one of you dies. Now I am not kidding. If you can't get through the gatekeeper, just keep trying.

Level with the gatekeeper. Before you abandon an attempted connection, level with the gatekeeper. "You know, Caleb, I've been trying to reach your boss for seventeen weeks now, and she just won't call me back. What should I do?" Give Caleb a chance to give you his advice, which may be a different way to connect with the boss, or even a referral down to some other person in the organization.

I once interviewed a top sales pro who made his entire living with the following technique: He would call a company's main phone line and say, "I need to know the name of the secretary or personal assistant to the CEO. What is his name and how do you spell that?" Then he would say, "Can you put me through to the CEO's office, please?" By asking for the office instead of the CEO herself, he almost always got put through. Let's say the CEO's personal assistant's name is Caleb. Then the rest of the technique works like this:

"Hello, Caleb. This is Alexander Slotnik. I don't think I really need to talk to the CEO. What I need to know about is _____. Who should I talk to about that? Who handles that type of thing?"

Caleb, being relieved that Mr. Slotnik is basically volunteering to be screened, and knowing that he is doing his duty to protect the CEO, sends Mr. Slotnik to someone else in the company.

Then Slotnik dials up that person's office and says, "Caleb, the personal assistant to the CEO, suggested that I talk to your boss about _____." Note that this is absolutely true.

Talk about borrowing authority! No personal assistant or secretary in any organization is going to cross the personal assistant or secretary to the CEO. Mr. Slotnick gets put through.

These techniques are all suitable for a family publication. You should try them out at some point in your job search. Mr. Slotnik's technique is a bit advanced, but the rest of them should become part of your tool kit. It would be a good idea to try them out before you really need them. Practice them on a contact who is not critical to your efforts. This is sales. You're selling you. And you darn sure want to make those calls if it will eradicate world hunger.

Your Goal Will Evolve

As you progress in your search, your goal with each of your contacts will evolve from simply getting information to having telephone conversations to meeting with people for casual chats to structured informational interviews to actually interviewing for a known opening. Your call to action will evolve to match your goals.

Your first endeavor is to get used to talking to people about your job search at all, even if you're wearing a pink bathrobe in your back yard at six in the morning. Your next goal is to explore your job ideas, to test them and make sure that they are sound. Then you'll be on the hunt for hiring authorities and direct referral sources. Once you have targets who are in the industry that you want to be in, you'll want to have more and more face-to-face meetings. Two minutes with a direct referral source is better than a phone call. And when it comes to hiring authorities, you want to have an informational interview if you have no other option, but you would prefer to interview as a "candidate-in-waiting" or as someone offering consulting solutions to a specific, known problem.

You have to go along with the flow as it develops. You're going to have some contacts who want to meet with you when you can't see the value of it. My suggestion: go to the meeting. You're going to get to say, "Who do you know who would know anything about _____?" while looking someone in the eye. You're going to get to practice your story. You're going to get to practice wearing your business clothes. Unless you have to buy an airplane ticket, go to any and all meetings.

A Suggestion

Finally, I want to add to my disclaimer provided early in the book that this guide is not for everyone. Not every technique suggested in this book should be used by every candidate or in every case. You have to use your own judgment about when to withhold a technique. Definitely you want to be more aggressive than you probably ever thought was appropriate. **You should be uncomfortable or you're probably not doing it right.**

However, different fields have different practices and norms. The way people get hired as a college professor is different from the way someone gets hired as a sales manager. Academia has a very old-fashioned approach to hiring. Academics like to hire someone they already know, but they also like to hire people who are almost Victorian in their formality. So being overly aggressive can be a turnoff, for a young academic. When applying for a job in almost all other settings, being overly enthusiastic and persistent is a plus. So you have to know your market.

Listen to the people you're talking with as you conduct your search. They'll let you know the limits of acceptable behavior. Then your job is to go as close to those limits as possible. And never slavishly accept the advice, "Just apply online." That's not good advice anywhere—unless you can hack the software and select yourself as the best candidate.

12

HOW to BREAK INTO ORGANIZATIONS

Breaking Down the Door

Your 100 leads will include a mix of possible organizations you'd like to work for and people you believe can lead you to those organizations. Your lead list will inevitably include some companies to which you simply cannot find an entrée: you don't know anybody there, and no friend of a friend or colleague of a colleague can be found. In this chapter we'll explore some ways to get in through the front door, the side door, the back door, or down the chimney. Even when you know someone at a targeted company, you should use the techniques in this chapter to approach other people at the company. You should go ahead and seek other channels, especially when you've gone as far as you can with your initial contact. If he can't put you in front of an interested hiring authority, try another route.

Think of an organization as a safe house in a zombie movie. You are the zombie invasion trying to break into the company headquarters, coming in at every door and window—and down the air vents! Trying, trying, trying to break in, relentless and tireless and everywhere at once.

I think you get the point: you are going to attack an organization through multiple channels. You're going to apply online. You're going to see if you have a connection to someone on the inside. You're going to write to people you identify at the firm. You're going to walk up to the building and ask to fill out an application. You're going to put your resume under the windshield wipers of all the executive cars in the parking lot. You're going to start hanging out in the nearest bar, or having coffee every morning in the nearest coffee shop.

You may have dozens of networking contacts and dozens of applications in play with some organizations you've targeted as highly desirable. Read the following sentence twice: I've actually had clients continue to receive rejection letters from employers as much as six months after they began to work there. They had so many applications pending through HQ and branches and different departments that they were earning a paycheck for months before they got the final ding letter!

Remember, you're going to be applying whether they have an opening or not. You've already gone to LinkedIn and tried to activate any connections you may have there. You've already checked your alumni database to see if anyone from your university works there. You've already begun to ask everyone you know if they know anyone at the organization, or anything about the organization.

One of the best ways to approach a company is a good, old-fashioned frontal assault. Check the HR portion of their website, and submit a resume online. This has a low chance of success, but you should do it anyway. Then, check the rest of the website and look for people with an email address or a query form. Email them or query them, "I am interested in working for your organization in _____ capacity. Who would I talk to about that? What's the best way to connect with someone in your company who would know about staffing needs in this area?"

Again, be highly specific. If you say you want to be a cost accountant specializing in progress payments for ongoing construction projects, they might think for a minute about how to help you. If you say you want "something in accounting," that's not going to have as high a response rate.

You will fail 99 percent of the time. You'll be ignored or told to apply online for the overwhelming percentage of attempts, but remember, a job search is a unique sales campaign. You only need one "yes." To be totally successful, you don't need to be successful for but a tiny fraction of your attempts. Expect to fail and you won't be disappointed, and failure will keep you at the task until you get the tips you need.

Here are more variants on this: if you are a college student or graduate student, you can write to *anyone you can find* and ask him the name and contact information for the "college relations manager" (undergrad) or "MBA recruiter." Say something like this: "I am a college senior majoring in music. Last summer I interned with a concert production company in St. Louis. I am interested in joining your company after I graduate. May I know the name of the college relations manager or the specific person who would make the decision to hire someone like me?"

Campus recruiters, undergrad and grad, specialize by function and/or region. For example, they may only recruit accounting and finance hires, or they only recruit from seven Midwestern states, and so on. It's great to be some kind of student, because most companies do not work to hide the identity of their campus recruiting officers. If you ask someone who knows, she'll usually give them up. Once you get the name, obviously, you'll reach out to him with an email and an appropriate call to action. Even if there's no job match at the moment, insist that you'd like to chat or meet with the recruiter as a "candidate-in-waiting."

If you're not a student, you can ask a very similar question: you can ask for the name of the technical recruiter, the professional recruiter, the management-level recruiter, or whatever most closely matches your situation. Please note that this puts you into hiring process *after a position has already been requisitioned,* but it's still more effective than dropping your resume into the black hole of an online submission app. You don't need to be coy. "May I know the name of the management recruiter who would handle someone such as myself?" or "May I know who in the company would be in charge of hiring someone like me?"

It is appropriate to send emails like this to anyone in any organization: "I am a Microsoft Certified Solutions Developer (MCSD), and I am interested in working for your company. Would you be so kind as to let me know of anyone in your work unit who hires or supervises tech people like me? I've already applied online and I've already written to the CIO, but I wonder if you know of anyone who is closer to the work-unit level, someone who would know about an opening or a project that's maybe behind schedule where I could help out. Any advice you can share with me would be greatly appreciated."

Your goal is to turn a company into a name into a referral into an appointment. Companies can't hire you; only people can. You will note that this process inserts you inside the organization ahead of a new job going through the HR process of requisition, skills analysis, drafting of a formal job description, and posting the opening to attract hundreds of candidates.

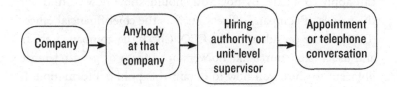

Your goal at this point is to have conversations of any kind with a hiring authority or first-line supervisor, the specific person who would be in charge of you if you were to be hired there. **You get jobs by talking to people.** Your job as a job seeker is to talk to the appropriate people.

Depending on the opportunity and where you are in your own career explorations, you can ask for informational interviews or consideration as a candidate-in-waiting. This process will also turn up openings for which the organization has an active search right now and, of course, you will apply for all of those following the instructions and advice of your contacts.

Timing matters. You don't have to do everything all at once. You might not want to send 200 emails into an organization on the same day. That might alarm people if they start comparing notes at the water cooler. But you have 100 leads at all times. So you can nibble away, incessantly, sending four and ten emails a week to various people in an organization, until you get the information or referrals that you want.

I hope you remember how to manage your tickle systems, as you have very complex communications going on. You need to track who you mailed to and when. You might want to review chapter 6, Managing Hundreds of Leads, pages 77–80.

You May Not Need a Name After All, and Consider Snail Mail and Even Fax Delivery

You don't always have to have a name to use this technique of applying for a *type of job* instead of an opening. Sometimes you can apply to a title. By now you should know how to find out the names of company officers, such as the chief financial officer (CFO) or the president or the CEO. Check the company website and use a data source like hoovers or zapdata or get a reference librarian to show you how to obtain this public information. If you're not a senior person, however, you might not find success applying four and five levels above your intended work unit. You may need to apply to someone in the middle of the organization. You can't always find out the name of the "regional controller" or the "head of customer service," but you can apply to those people, without a name, by writing to them *by title* in the good old-fashioned snail mail. This is a classic application, a cover letter sent in with a resume. This works, but it's not ideal. This is not a preferred technique. This is what you do when you can't find any other entrée or introduction into an organization. Note that this does get you into the game ahead of any posted openings.

If you can't find specific hiring authorities, you apply to a title, instead of a known person. For example, law, accounting, and some consulting firms have a senior person who takes care of hiring and staffing. This person is called the "hiring partner." So if you want a job at a law, an accounting, or a consulting firm, you can send your materials in to the hiring partner, and you've successfully applied and avoided the whole "apply online" runaround.

These organizations are often fairly small, a few dozen people at the branch level. That's why this technique works. In a national HQ setting, your missive might be lost or placed in a stack multiple inches thick every single day. In a smaller setting your missive lands on the right desk, even if you don't know the name of the person you're writing to.

Though fax machines are obsolete, most offices still have them. Consider faxing in your application. It's different. It shows a sense of urgency. It gets you out of the resume pile.

Here's a success story: a client was out of work, but she was very shy. She wanted to work in accounting in the financial district of San Francisco. She knew what she wanted to do and where she wanted to do it, so those were counts in her favor. The fact that she was very shy created a roadblock. I have a retired legal secretary who sometimes does administrative work for me and my clients on an as-needed basis. *She is not shy.* She called all the most prestigious independent CPA firms in the financial district and asked, "May I know your fax number please?" Not one single firm refused to give out its fax number. She followed that up with, "May I know the name of the hiring partner, please?" She asked this in a smooth and even tone, as if this were the most normal query in the world. Nevertheless, only about half would give her a specific name.

My client and I prepared only a couple of dozen applications, about half to a specific person and half just addressed to "Hiring Partner." Each letter was fully customized. Accounting firms are conservative and traditional, so we made each letter a full business letter, and faxed it in followed by her one-page resume. She received several calls but only one interview. Fortunately, it was at the most prestigious boutique accounting firm in San Francisco, a firm specializing in taxation for high-net-worth families and their complex affiliated partnerships, estates, and trusts. They have clients all over the world. She interviewed with the hiring partner in the morning, went to lunch with three partners, and had an offer by telephone late in the afternoon.

The entire time of her search was one week. We spent one meeting planning and positioning her candidacy, and one meeting preparing her resume. My research assistant spent part of one day building her target list of firms, hiring partners, and fax numbers. We spent an hour or two faxing the letters and resumes out. She went to one interview. Unemployed to employed in one week.

Here's another success story, I just received last week via email: "I went to my local library to pick up a copy of your book, *How to Get Any Job: Career Launch and Re-launch for Everyone Under 30 (or how to avoid living in your parents' basement).*" That's the college version of current theories on the job market and career choice, and a companion to this book in your hands.

"It was so good I checked it out of the library twice, and then ordered my own copy. This means that in my mind, your work is on par with Sartre and Shakespeare, as I almost never buy books." Words like these would melt any writer's heart.

"I took your advice in looking for an internship between my junior and senior years. I found a career role model, who does communications and marketing for a liberal arts college, and thought to myself, 'How would I go about doing that for a living?'

"I wrote about forty letters to public relations professionals at various colleges and universities in my area asking for a summer internship. About ten of them got back to me, often just to say that they were impressed with my resume and were sorry that they couldn't hire a summer intern. One hired me. As you always say, you only need one! While many of my friends were floundering around this past summer, I had a paid job doing work that interested me, writing and redeveloping a law school's website."

The point for us here is "forty letters" equaled "one job." Don't wait for an opening to be announced, for the sad privilege of competing with hundreds of other people. Get out there and apply for a *type of job* and, whenever possible, apply to a specific person as near to the work-unit level as possible. This inserts you into the process at the point—in both time and space—where and when a job is created. You're the default candidate. You're already in the mind of the decision maker when she decides to hire. You are at the front of the line.

Most important of all: you're involved well ahead of the requisition-skills analysis-job description-posted-opening process that so hinders your ability to get that job.

Here's another success story: Maureen Dawes wanted to work in commercial real estate in California, and she was open to living anywhere from San Diego to the Oregon border. She built by hand a list of the 200 largest and/or most dynamic real estate development and consulting firms in the state. From their websites she identified two senior people in each firm. That's 400 people. Then she began to methodically email to those 400 people every two weeks. After the first mailing, she began all the continuing emails with "I've updated my resume since we last had contact. Attached is the new version. I'm still interested in real estate development or consulting. Let me know if anything comes to mind. Thank you for your help!"

I insisted that she actually change the resume each time if she was going to use this technique, because I think it is important never to tell a lie. So she did. Some of the changes were very minor. Sometimes she put her middle initial in, and sometimes she took it out. But there was always some change.

She knew a handful of the 400 people already, so they quickly offered her up some tips and leads, but what was fascinating was that she began to get tips, leads, referrals, and interviews from many of the random strangers she was emailing. I'm convinced that some of them began to believe that they knew her!

How to Apply for a Posted Opening

When you see an attractive posted opening, apply for it, of course. Comply with the instructions in the posting for applying. At the same time, work your entire network to try to get a referral and any inside information on the company that will help you (a) be a better candidate, and (b) make sure you actually want to work there if offered the opportunity.

Go ahead and reach out to the hiring authority. You may want to apply online *and* try to get closer to the decision maker. If you can find out who is in charge of the hiring, go ahead and send her an email, in particular if you can establish a mutual acquaintance, a referral, or any other kind of connection. "I applied online. I know you may have many applicants for this position, and I just want to reach out to you and tell you of my sincere interest in this position and your organization. My resume and cover letter are attached, if you would have a moment to look at them. Let me know if you have any preliminary questions, and I hope to advance to the interview stage if you see a match." Nice, polite, and, unless they tell you not to do this, perfectly acceptable.

Deliver your application as close to the source as possible. If you can get your application hand delivered to the hiring authority by a current employee, that's ideal. If you find the job posted on a job board *and* on the company's website, apply on the company's website. They'll look there first, and may ignore feeds from the big national boards if they find who they want off their own site. Consider faxing your resume in addition to submitting it online. Finally, if it is really a perfect job for you, and you can discover the correct name of the hiring authority, consider sending in your application via overnight courier. Even executives will open their own packets from overnight couriers (FedEx, UPS, Airborne, and similar). Using an overnight courier all the time would be ridiculously expensive, but when you see a perfect match, it might be worth it.

Try to be referred by a current employee. Ask for referrals! It is fine to write to people who are in the same association as you who work at the company, or went to the same college as you and work at the same company, or go the same temple as you and work at the company, and so on. You can even contact total strangers who are in the same line of work as you if you can discover their email off the company website.

Brazenly ask them to refer you for the position. Why would they do this? Because a large number of employers give actual cash rewards, typically $50 to $300, to employees who refer new hires. Also, good employees want to work with other good employees, so if you are a good catch, they'll be interested in helping you get on with the company. Their reservation will be that you are a dud. If you give any hint of being a dud, this will not work.

Here's a sample email to someone who doesn't know you at all:

Hello, Mr. Dodson—

My name is Anya Madsen. I will be applying to your company for the position of senior account representative. I wonder if you would be so kind as to refer me for the opening. I've attached my resume for your consideration, and I've also included it in the body of this email beginning immediately after my signature line. You will know what it takes to be successful in your organization in a position like this, and I think I have what it takes. Your opinion will matter. Regardless of whether I am selected or not, I can promise to be interesting, well prepared, and professional as a candidate. I'd be happy to answer any questions you might have of me. The job code is Senior-CSR-3987/NJ2010.

Let me know if I can use your name as a referral.

Sincerely,
Anya Madsen

Most employees will ignore an email like this, but it doesn't cost you anything if they do. If you get a referral, great. If you don't, fine.

As mentioned earlier, employee referrals are favored in almost all resume database systems. Getting a referral is vastly superior to just throwing your resume into their database to fend for itself.

Use the words from the posting in your response. Rework your resume and letter for every application. Look at the posting and pull out all the unique words you find there. Look especially for unique nouns and phrases, like "floating-point scheduling" or

"Zenon4 App Suite" or "Hungarian." Then put these in your resume. Resumes get separated from cover letters, so make sure anything important is in your resume itself.

Mention their competitors. Employers search for resumes with their competitors names in them. So make a list of their competitors and find ways to mention them in your resume. A clever person can find ways to put virtually anything into his resume. There are many ways to insert phrases like "Report to a C-level officer" and "fluent in Chinese" besides knowing how to say "knee how!" to the CIO. For more on this, see *The Overnight Resume,* a companion guide to this book.

Be a local. If the job is in Houston, put Houston on your resume heading. Omit the rest of the heading that indicates you're living in Casper, Wyoming. You can omit street address, phone number, everything but name, city, email:

Heather Montoya
Houston, Texas
heather291@gmail.com

Obviously, you would only do this if you are ready and able to move to Houston in a quick hurry. Employers search for city names, zip codes, and area codes. A clever resume writer can find ways to get all of these into a document.

Always include the job code. When there is a job code you should always include it in all communiqués. It can be part of the heading for either email or snail mail, or in the subject line of an email. Without that code, you're just another random piece of spam.

Be careful with online applications and profiles. You will often be asked to fill out online applications and profiles on the company's HR site. These may include requests for all types of personal information that you are uncomfortable giving out at such a preliminary stage. You may run into requests for information about your work unit, who was your boss, references, phone numbers, reasons for leaving, all kinds of information that you should not give out to strangers. Never, ever give out information that you think could be used to scam you (see the next section, below), in particular, date of birth and Social Security number! Skip windows requesting overly personal information if the program will let you or, if it won't, put in gibberish. Try entering stuff like "%providelater&" or "#bring2interview*" and similar.

Then wait. Beyond all this, when there is a posted opening, you can definitely overdo it. Companies are slow to hire. They may collect resumes for weeks, then do nothing for weeks, then interview a few people and not like any of them, then start over. So put your contact on a tickle list for every ten days or so, but more than that could put you in the "trouble" file. See chapter 13, Staying Alive, beginning on page 181.

Fake Job Postings, Fake People, Fake Headhunters, Identity Theft, Scams

I hate to tell you this, but there are evil people out there preying upon job seekers, and there are some corporate practices that are injurious and insensitive to job seekers. Posted openings are their main way of attracting their victims.

For example, some job postings you will see are fake. There is no opening at all—the company or the search firm is simply building their resume databank. They know that sooner or later they'll need people with the skills advertised, but they're not hiring right now. They're trying to get out ahead of the process for some future need. Some companies even use job postings to psych out their competition, make them think they're launching a product line or going in one direction with R&D when they are in fact not.

Unscrupulous companies use job postings as a cheap and dirty way to run a salary survey. If you see "responses without salary history will not be considered," then it's very likely that the company is not really looking for the engineer—or what have you—that they posted. They're just doing a salary survey without paying for it. Never provide salary information in a first response to a job advertisement of any kind, no matter what they say in a posting. Just write "salary history provided upon interview" or if it is part of an online form, try skipping that window. If you can't skip it, try putting in a zero or typing in "on interview." If they give you a table to pick values from, for example, "❏ $41–50K ❏ $51–60K ❏ $61–70K" and so on, again, try to skip it. If it won't let you skip it, just mark the lowest possible value.

By the way, this goes for "salary desired" tables also. Providing any type of salary information before an interview is not in your best interests. Any kind. If they won't call you because you didn't provide salary information *they weren't going to call you anyway.*

Although I will admit that I have a minority opinion on this, I do not think that job applicants should even give out their mailing address on Internet applications. Your name, email address, and cell phone are sufficient contact information for any legitimate hiring organization (with the exception of government entities who may insist on more). If the street address portion of the online form can't be skipped, just type in "provide on interview."

As mentioned in an earlier section, you can even withhold your real name from a first-stage contact. If your name is "Ruth" and you've always fancied the name "Clarissa," and your last name is "Johnson" and you've always thought it would be nice to have a more exotic name like "Salvatore," then by all means look for work using the name "Clarissa Salvatore." This is particularly germane if you are currently employed. To go totally anonymous, see *The Overnight Resume* for more on those techniques. You need to be ready to explain why you felt the need to be anonymous, but there are certainly good reasons for choosing to withhold your full identity, especially when you are unsure of their full identity!

Think I'm paranoid? A "company" in Tennessee set up a fake hiring office in a hotel room and invited applicants in for a personal interview. They processed more than a thousand applications requesting full name, date of birth, Social Security number, mother's maiden name, other names ever used, all addresses over the past five years, and so on. The whole thing was a criminal operation to set up identity theft scams. If you're suspicious, don't provide the information. Real companies seeking good employees will not insist on such information before an offer is made.

In addition to fake ads, there are fake people. It is perfectly legal in the United States to advertise jobs using a fake contact name. This allows companies to run ads saying "Apply to Susan Scott at this address," but there is no Susan Scott. If you call for Susan Scott, they know you're a job applicant. This is just something to be aware of.

And as you pursue a job, there will be scamsters pursuing you. You will receive queries that purport to be from headhunters. Some of these are bait-and-switch games, where you respond, then they say they're really an "executive marketing firm." They would be happy to help you put yourself on the market in a more professional manner. They love to say that they have thousands of invisible leads in the hidden job market. The fee is only $4,000 or $7,000 or $15,000, and wouldn't it be worth it to you to get a new job right away? Scam!

If they contact you, instead of you contacting them, that's your first warning sign. If anyone promises you a job or says this whole job change thing can be easy, that's a huge warning sign. You cannot write a check and get a job. No one, not even executives with plenty of money, can delegate or buy a package job search. Job search is not easy, and no amount of wishing will make it so. Be smart and avoid scams.

More Proper and More Creative Cover Letters

The rest of this chapter is a series of ideas for contacting organizations when you don't have an inside introduction. Most of the time, you will want to be sending these letters to the hiring authority closest to the job you want; if you're in nursing you'd be writing to the head of nursing, not the chief of the hospital. If you're interested in being a loan officer, you'd want to find and mail to some branch managers, not the VP of HR for the East Coast.

Consider using snail mail for some of your queries, especially when contacting employers where you don't have a personal referral. Providing a well-crafted and well-presented cover letter and resume is a demonstration of your business skills. Also, misaddressed or poorly addressed snail mail usually gets delivered to somebody, but a bad email address sends your letter straight to nowhere forever.

Snail mail is a curiosity, these days. It's unusual. It takes milliseconds for an HR manager to delete or forward your email missive into the resume capture system. It takes much longer to open, glance at, and dispose of a real letter and resume. Whenever you snail mail a resume, offer to send an e-version if they would prefer it. Just write at the bottom of your cover letter or resume (or both), "If you would like an e-version of these documents, just email me at you@yourmail.com, and I'll send them promptly by return email."

If you're going to write to the same people several times, which I strongly recommend, then mix up your emails and your snail mails. Give them a different look at you.

Unfortunately, I've noticed that people are losing the ability to write and design a business letter. See *The Overnight Resume Guide* for full-size examples.

Whenever you can, **write to people—not companies, titles, or departments.** When you can't discover the people, then of course you *do* write to companies, titles, or departments.

Write a straightforward, no-nonsense letter. You don't need to be Shakespeare. A bad cover letter used often is better than an outstanding cover letter used seldom. So, don't worry about being a clever writer. People want to know your skills. As long as you are clear about what kind of job you're seeking and what skills you have to apply on such a job, they're not worried about whether you're a "writer" or not.

However, I do think that you can improve response rates by using more creative letters, especially when you are writing to an organization without a personal referral of any kind. You have to stand out a bit to gain attention from people who are not running an active job search, and have no reason to give you part of their day.

I love letters that use a hook line. In advertising, a hook line is those very few words, usually large and in bold, that get you to read the rest of the advertisement. Hook lines don't need to be questions, but I think questions are particularly effective, for example, "Would You Do This to Your Kids?"

Here's another example: "Will all your projects stay on track this summer during the hectic vacation season? Do you have some special projects you'd love to get launched? Perhaps I can help. I am a first-year MBA candidate with an unusually strong work background, and I am seeking a summer internship with your organization."

I also like letters that begin with the second person. "You're probably upset about the recent changes in tax policy." It takes a special skill to write in the second person without offending people. You have to think like they think, anticipate their concerns, and voice those concerns in a way that is neither condescending nor off-key.

Here's an example email in which the candidate uses hook lines in the second person. This candidate is seeking an international assignment. Even if the recipient had no pending needs for an international sales rep, if she thought she were at all interested in opening European markets *at any time in the future,* she'd be likely to talk to the candidate. Also notice the aggressive call to action.

Attn: Charyn Soldano, VP of Sales & Business Development
Re: Europe

Dear Ms. Soldano:

Are your customers in Europe totally happy with you? Are there markets you have not opened because you don't have the internal resources to open them? For my last employer, I increased European revenues by $15 million in just two years by improving relations with existing accounts. I would be delighted to have the opportunity to make such a contribution to your organization.

Perhaps you will find this of interest:

- Virtually my entire career history has been in international marketing and key account services, with the last seven years in Europe, Latin America, the Far East, South Africa, and Australia.

- Fluent in English, French, Spanish, Italian; proficient in German.

- Available 100% for business travel or relocation anywhere in the world.

- Strategic, analytical, planning skills. Can develop fully justified/ supported customer support plans to meet your needs globally and by region/country.

I am very interested in discussing this further with you, first by telephone and if we can establish a mutual interest, then in person. I will call you before five o'clock tomorrow afternoon to see if you have a moment to chat with me. I hope you'll remember my name so you can take the call. Or you can contact me 24/7 at 4newmarkets@ mgmt.topten.edu or 212-555-0920.

Thank you for your consideration. I look forward to our conversation!

My warmest regards,
Valeria Carla Firenza

Letters that grab a news item and relate it to the employer's concerns can be very effective. This shows you pay attention to the news, for one thing. It shows you pay attention to their concerns, as well. It creates urgency and currency, as in being "up to the moment."

Here's an example opening for a letter tied to a news item:

Today's headline in the *Wall Street Journal* is "Some economists see roaring recovery. Better-than-expected data support optimists." Are you going to have the management infrastructure in place to maximize your company's benefit from recovery? I would like to be part of your company's success in the coming boom. Please consider the following . . .

Another type of cover letter is called the **broadcast cover letter.** That's when you write to employers and offer to solve a particular kind of problem for them. You are announcing to the world that you have a specific expertise, such as the ability to migrate systems from the old software suite Alpha to the new, improved software suite Beta. If you build a careful target list of hiring authorities at employers where that skill should be of value, then this can be quite successful. It is irrelevant whether these employers have an open requisition to hire or not. If you can build a list of companies that are highly likely to have a problem you can resolve, then you're in business (in some cases, literally).

Here is an example of a broadcast cover letter. It is for someone relatively early in her career, seeking access to a specific type of employer. The letter shows an aggressive call to action; the writer is going to be calling to follow up. Letters like these have to be sent over and over again, like Maureen Dawes and her 400 contacts in commercial real estate (see page 157). Don't worry about someone being annoyed with receiving your letter every week. Remember, a job search is a unique campaign. You're not trying to make 100 new friends; you're trying to get *one person* to talk to you in his office.

Also, each email must be to a specific person—even if you send the same letter to a thousand people a week. Mass mailings aren't usually effective even when they do get lucky and slip past spam filters.

TO: alan.jones@financialservices.com
SUBJECT: Research to support high-end customers' account management strategies

Attn: Alan Jones
Senior Investment Advisor
Jones, Smith, Wallace & Hart Investment Advisors
Atlanta, Georgia

Dear Mr. Jones:

This is not spam or bot-mail. This is an actual person writing directly to you, one-to-one. Give me a chance to offer you a way to build closer bonds with your most valuable accounts. This is a short email, and you'll know by the bottom if this idea would make you money.

Do you ever wish you could have someone on your staff who could help you develop compelling visual stories to go with your compelling investment strategies?

Have you ever given a presentation to a high-net-worth family representative to have him say to you, "Yeah, but I'd need to see the research on that." Do you always have the specific research that would persuade him?

I'm obsessed with investment research, modeling, investment theories, investor decision making, and similar arcane subjects. Even more important than that, I can turn analysis into accessible reports, full-color charts and graphs, financial stories in numbers and visuals that can help you get your ideas across to your most important accounts.

I'd love to be working in your office producing these reports, analyses, and visuals. If you have the top-end clients I think you do, then I'm absolutely confident that I can provide value.

Can we talk? I'll ring you tomorrow morning before noon. If that's not good for you, email me and let me know when is best for you.

Eager to connect,
Adisson Pattelmek

Note that the call to action is for a conversation, *not to interview for a job*. If you're simply too shy to cold call someone, you can use a call to action like this: "Email me and let me know it's okay to call you, and let's get this ball rolling."

I don't know how to drive this home except to say it over and over again: these letters are like advertisements; you can send them to the same people every week to ten days until you get a job. These letters are like advertisements; you can send them to the same people every week to ten days until you get a job. These letters are like advertisements; you can send them to the same people every week to ten days until you get a job.

Repetition drives response. You're not going to run out and buy a new Mercedes the first time you see a Mercedes advertisement that interests you, are you? These broadcast letters work the same way. People see your name and your pitch several times. It appears to be a one-to-one email, from you to them, unique each time. "Mr. Barton, I know you haven't responded to my prior two emails. I'm hoping this one catches your eye. This is not spam. It's a note from me to you." Don't send it every day, because that steps deep into nasty annoying territory, but every week or ten days and you're like McDonald's. You start to own some mindshare.

Finally, for people who have some rare or special expertise, offering your services in a **consulting cover letter** is the apex of frontal assaults. It gives you a great rationale for meeting face to face: you think you can solve a particular problem for them as a consultant. You're not looking for a job so much as an engagement. Of course, if they like the service you provide on the consulting engagement, you're first in line if a related opening develops.

You don't have to be a senior person to use this technique. I interviewed a college student who sent out fliers to local businesses: "I will fix one problem on your laptop absolutely for free, to introduce my IT support services to you." It gave him access to people who never would have talked to him as a job seeker, and resulted in his being hired for a position that had, ironically, nothing to do with technology.

There comes a time in an extended job search when you have to get something new to put on your resume anyway, so this consulting pitch really serves two purposes at once. It gives you a more effective way to get into people's offices, and it keeps your skills fresh.

If you've been in the job market for some time with little success, I am strongly advocating that you reposition your search to use this consulting methodology. Done right, it will get you talking to the right people. If you are a senior person out of work for more than a year, you have to consider starting a business or starting a consulting practice. It's the honorable thing to do. You may be a reluctant entrepreneur, but otherwise you're going to become a reluctant retiree. Educate yourself on how to start and run a small business, which is very different from being the boss of a work unit or a whole company.

Here's an example of a consulting pitch letter:

Subject: High-Net-Worth Clients and New Business

Dear Ms. Kline:

Is your sales model leaving money on the table? The problem is hard to see, sometimes. You know what your sales force is generating, sure, but does it haunt you what they're missing?

So maybe they're bringing you some new revenue, short of your goals, but close enough to keep things going, *but are they walking right over the top of much greater potential?* It's like they see the dollar on top of the ground, but not what's buried underneath their feet.

You know the market is out there. You suspect that they're chipping away at it, but not grabbing the thing whole. Fishing for perch and not for whales, blaming the economy, settling for less than stellar numbers.

By the way, it doesn't mean there's anything wrong with your sales staff. It doesn't mean that your best new accounts rep is not doing his or her job. But your sales model might need a tune-up.

I want to offer you some free consulting. I want to offer you better access to high-net-worth clients. They make decisions differently. They're not driven by price but by features. They're not interested in discounts, but value. They don't mind if you have higher margins if you are attentive to their best interest.

I can deliver these clients to you. There are several ways I can do it, and that's why I'd like to chat about your sales model and what you're doing now.

May we have a discussion about this? I'll ring you in the next twenty-four hours to see if this is of potential interest to you. Whether you decide to engage me or not, I think you'll enjoy the conversation, and begin to see revenue potential in a whole new light.

Take a look at the attachment if you get a chance. I think you'll like what you see. You don't need to ring me. I'll be in touch soon.

Kindest regards,
R. Wilson Smith

You will notice that Wilson Smith uses a very aggressive call to action. If you send queries like this, then you absolutely must have 100 percent execution and follow-through. For those of you who are shy, a "safer" call to action may be: "Email me and let me know it's okay to call you." That's a pretty easy phone call to make, but even then you may have to call them over and over to connect. If you have too much trouble connecting, you may revert to email to close an appointment to meet with them: "Coleman, I just can't seem to catch you by phone. I've called several times, but only left a couple of messages. Let's set a time to meet in person, if that's all right with you. Would Tuesday morning at 10 A.M. work for you, or is sometime Wednesday better?"

That's a classic **A-B Split.** In an A-B Split, you offer your correspondent a choice, A or B, either of which you would be delighted to have also. You can do this orally or in writing—it's an effective technique in either medium. Choice A should be more precise and more proximate than the second choice. Since more people are in their office on Tuesday morning than any other day of the week, "Tuesday at 10 A.M." is a great first choice. Choice B should be vague and further out, and harder to give a blanket rejection to, as in, "or is later in the week better for you?"

As mentioned earlier, avoid asking yes-no questions in any sales situation. Ask open-ended questions that can only benefit you, or use the A-B Split technique. Here's an open-ended question: "What's a better time for me to reach you?" This is an entirely different question than "Can I call you back another time?" Do you see the difference?

Any version of this sentence is a good A-B Split: "Would you like to get together first thing Monday morning, or is later in the week better?"

There are a couple more techniques to discover hiring authorities inside organizations where you have no connection: The Postcard Technique and the Senior Survey.

The Postcard Technique is labor-intensive and a bit expensive per contact, but is shockingly effective. Write a snail-mail letter to employers and ask them who hires someone like you. Describe yourself and what kind of job you are interested in, *but do not send a resume.* You can write to a person, if you can find a name and title, or even to a department if you can't find any contact information at all. In your letter, you enclose a self-addressed, stamped postcard. This is a very special postcard.

On the front of the card, you have the correct postage and your own address on a label (the card is addressed to you). On the back of the card, you have invited the contact to give you instructions for how best to engage with the organization. Be sure to write your contact's name and address either on the front as the return address or on the back as in the example below. Otherwise, you're not going to know who sent it to you! A little sense of humor never hurts, as well. Nobody is going to check box number three.

FROM
Maria Gonzales, V.P. of Export Sales
XYZ Corporation
505 Main Street
Bentonville, Arkansas 72731 USA

Please check one and return this self-addressed stamped postcard to the address as marked on the other side. Thank you!

☐ Yes, I'd be willing to discuss our hiring plans and processes. I can be reached at this telephone number _____, ext. _____, or you can email me at my direct email address _____.

☐ I've forwarded your materials to _____. You can mention my name when you contact him/her directly at this telephone number _____, ext. _____, or via email at _____.

☐ Don't contact us further! We'd *never* hire someone like you! Go away!

You may be asking yourself: Hey, if Don Asher tells people to do this in bestselling books, then hasn't this already been done to death? The answer is, no. This is an entirely novel practice. Most people don't use snail mail at all in a job search, much less something as elaborate as this. Few people are willing to do the work that it takes to implement this system. You have to research companies and identify contacts. You have to go to an office supply store and buy blank postcards. You have to run the postcards through a laser printer, and they almost always jam. You have to put labels and postage on return cards, many of which you know will not be coming back to you. That feels wasteful to many people. Finally, you're reading this on page 174 of this book. It's in the back of the book intentionally. You're one of the people who has not given up and gone back to applying online, furtively, in the middle of the night. You're one of the readers who is going to master the HJM system of applying for jobs before they're posted. This system is a jewel.

There are some variations on the technique. To do it in large volumes, a copy center can print the basic postcards in bulk. Their equipment is designed to handle such cards. By using stick-on labels for outgoing and return addresses, you reduce hassle and can manage mass, customized mailings. Using labels does reduce response. My clients have proven that by testing it both ways. There's something about that postcard being printed custom that causes people to respond.

Some of my workshop attendees have put this line in their letter: "If it is to your greater convenience to give me a call or email me a response, please advise me at (310) 555-2042 or via dave8934@gmail.com." I'm against this practice. It removes the novelty factor, and makes the return postcard and postage superfluous. I have not run any study to prove whether it hurts response rates, but it is my counsel to stick to the original system. As hokey as it may be, it could be that its very hokey-ness is what makes it effective.

Some of my senior clients have modified the system so that the postcards are not mailed back, but are put in self-addressed, stamped envelopes (SASE). One client said, "At my level, the people I'm writing to are not going to want to mail their contact information exposed on a postcard where everybody can see that. They're going to want some privacy." Valid enough. You can get return envelopes, size #9, at any major office supply store.

The final technique I want to suggest to you is the **Senior Survey.** It was originally designed for college seniors to use to explore the job market in their areas of interest, and to build a bridge between the college experience and the world of work. It can also be used by job club members, but to much less effect. Students are like puppies and kittens. Everybody loves students. They don't so much love job seekers.

The senior survey should be sent via email using the three-shot system. If the contact ignores the survey three times by email, it can then be printed up and sent to her in the good old-fashioned snail mail. If you claim you are doing this for a class, it had better be true! Go see the professor and get her blessing for this project. You're bound to improve your grade, plus improve your chances of gaining employment out of college.

Attn: LaShondra Washington, Principal
Washington & Associates Media & Communication Specialists

Ms. Washington:

I am a senior at Oklahoma State University, and I am conducting a research project to survey employers in media, advertising, and public relations in the Oklahoma City area. My goal is to improve the match between employers' needs and student expectations. The result of my survey will be presented to my senior seminar class in the School of Communications.

Would you please take just a moment to help me? If you would fill out the following questionnaire and return it to me, I would be very appreciative. All you have to do is hit "reply" to this email, and give your responses. Thank you!!!

1. Does your company ever hire new college graduates?
❑ Yes ❑ No

2. If yes, for what positions or types of positions?

3. Do you hire undergraduate interns?
❑ Yes ❑ No ❑ We'd consider it

4. Do you hire post-baccalaureate interns?
❑ Yes ❑ No ❑ We'd consider it

5. Do you hire graduate interns?
❑ Yes ❑ No ❑ We'd consider it

6. Which of the following skills, talents, traits, and abilities are very important to you in a new hire?

❑ A positive attitude and a good nature.
❑ The ability to answer the phone in a professional manner.
❑ The ability to take direction and follow instructions.
❑ The ability to work directly with clients.
❑ Punctuality.
❑ Knowledge of standard office suites, including word processing applications.
❑ Knowledge of standard office suites, including spreadsheet applications.
❑ Computer skills in general.
❑ The ability to learn new computer skills without formal training.
❑ Programming experience.
❑ Skills in financial and statistical analysis.
❑ Professional dress.
❑ Customer service skills, including the ability to take a complaint.
❑ The ability to make a presentation to a group.
❑ The ability to write well.
❑ Sales talent, in the sense of managing existing relationships.
❑ Sales talent, in the sense of coldcalling for new relationships.
❑ The ability to do practical research, to "find things out" on one's own.
❑ The ability to perform formal, library, database, and Internet research.

- ❑ Foreign languages, especially _____.
- ❑ Honesty and trustworthiness.
- ❑ The ability to make decisions with incomplete information.
- ❑ The ability to function on a team, and resolve minor interpersonal issues independently.
- ❑ Willingness to work overtime as needed.
- ❑ Negotiating talent.
- ❑ Ability to unjam a printer, copier, or fax without running for help.
- ❑ Ability to organize and plan work, including projects.
- ❑ Ability to train and motivate others.

7. Which of the above or other skills, talents, traits, and abilities are most important to you in a new hire?

8. What, in your opinion, are the best reasons to hire a less experienced person?

9. What do you find least appealing about new hires? What could they do better?

10. What is your "hiring cycle"? When do you first begin to look at student resumes for hiring each year's new crop of college graduates?
❑ Sep–Nov ❑ Dec–Jan ❑ Feb–Mar ❑ Apr–May ❑ Anytime

11. If you hire interns, when do you first begin to look at student resumes for summer interns?
❑ Sep–Nov ❑ Dec–Jan ❑ Feb–Mar ❑ Apr–May ❑ Anytime ❑ N/A

12. To which person and/or to what office do you prefer entry-level candidates apply?

Name_____

Title_____

Department_____

Address_____

13. Do you have any advice for me and my fellow students about to launch careers this year?

14. May we call you to discuss your hiring needs and processes further?

❏ Yes, call me at this number _____ or set up a call using this email:_____.

❏ It's better if you call this person:

Name_____

Title_____

Department_____

Number_____

Email _____

Thank you! Thank you! Thank you!

Cory Sanders
Student, OSU School of Communications

This survey form works best with smaller organizations or with specific departments within larger ones, and won't work at all if you send it to VPs of HR at Fortune 500 companies. As mentioned in an earlier section, with larger organizations you can still find someone interested in this survey by calling and asking for the name and address of the "College Relations Manager" serving your region or function. Fortune 500 companies will tell you who this is.

You can also conduct the survey by phone. Used correctly, this survey will work for undergraduate and graduate students in any major. "Hi. My name is George Plimpton and I am in a graduate seminar in journalism at Columbia University. I'm going to be giving a presentation on the country's top sports journalists, and I was wondering if you could take a moment and tell me how you got into the business." That's informational interviewing.

If you use this technique, make sure that you actually write the paper or give the presentation or do whatever it was you said you were going to do. You will in all likelihood shortly be contacting this person again to ask about concrete job opportunities, and she will almost certainly ask to see the paper or inquire how the presentation went. As I've said before, *never tell a lie in a career-related setting*. It's more than dishonest—it's a failure of creativity.

To use this system as a member of a job club, you would redesign the questions to reflect the level of work and worker in question, and change your instructions to read something like this: "I am a member of a job club, and many of us are interested in financial services positions. We are building a map of financial services firms and mid-level jobs in this area. I would be grateful if you would have just a few seconds to fill out the following questions and forward them to me. All you have to do is hit 'reply' to this email, and from there it's self-explanatory. Thank you so much for helping us out!"

The last chapter more fully explains job clubs and their advantages. Every job seeker should form or find a job club.

13

STAYING ALIVE

Hiring Takes Time

Hiring processes take time. Managers are in and out of the office. Key people travel. The requisition gets put on hold in some kind of budget fright, then revived when it becomes clear that the worker is badly needed after all. Other people in line for the job look better than you, but then they fail the drug test or tell a sexist joke. You rise up in the rankings, then fall back, then rise again. Maybe even someone else is hired, but he didn't show up on the first day, or he doesn't work out and is let go after eighty-nine days. The frustrating thing is that you can't see any of this from outside the organization.

Once you start to come under consideration for actual jobs, you should be ready to sustain your candidacy over a prolonged period of time. It can take months between the time a hiring authority says, "Yes, we're interested in you," and the time you might get to start a job.

If you don't get a ding letter, you keep your candidacy going. It's an open item, a "possible." Except for actual offers, this is the most important category you should be tracking.

Your goal is to occupy mental space in the brain of the hiring authority every week or two no matter how long it takes for her to either hire you or ding you. **Don't fade away!** And don't let her fade away, either. Just because you don't hear from her does not mean that you're not the first-choice candidate. It may mean she's busy or sidetracked.

Tickle your contact every ten days or so. "LaTonya, I'm just checking in to see if you're ready to move forward on the hiring project. I know you see a lot of people, so I'll remind you that you interviewed me for a patient records position. You were quite encouraging and told me to stay in touch, so I'm wondering what's next. Standing by, Jennifer Whatley."

Nice, polite, every week or two, until you either get hired or dinged. It takes some real cleverness to stay alive for months without becoming a nag or sounding petulant. Be creative in finding reasons to connect, and alternate your modes of contact. Send an email one week, send a card ten days after that, then leave a voice-mail, then start over with an email. Send a new reference. Update your resume and send a new version of your resume. Send an article or a human interest item. "I remember when we interviewed that you liked microlending. Here's an article about microlending in the Bronx! Imagine that. Let me know when you want to proceed with the interview process for the position we discussed. Standing by," etc., etc., etc.

Here's a version of a tickle called a **continuing interest letter.** You can send letters and emails like this several times, if you hear nothing from them.

Attn: Riaj Sahay
Re: Student Recruiting

Dear Riaj:

I spoke with you in June about the student recruiting position for the welding school in Scranton. I'm hoping that your company's plans have been progressing toward opening! I've left you some messages and sent you a new version of my resume, and I just wanted to let you know that I remain very interested in this oppor-tunity. I think I can bring a lot to this type of position, with my back-ground in trades and in secondary education. Please let me know if I am still a candidate and what I can do to help you decide whether there's a fit for me with your company.

Standing by,
Nash Potts

Never fade away. Make them either hire you or ding you.

Timing and Multiple Offers

When you start to get close to one offer, you can leverage your other open items. This is somewhat risky, because you can force someone to reject you who might have hired you if not pressed. For this reason, whenever you can control the timing, try to get your first offer from your first-choice opportunity.

Once you have an offer, or feel that you are about to have an offer, let all the organizations that are considering you know that you may soon be forced to make a decision:

> I just wanted to check in with you and let you know that I think I am about to get an offer from another company. I really liked the opportunity we discussed, and I would not like to be forced to make a decision before I know where we stand. Is it possible that we could accelerate your decision-making process? Let's chat by phone. I'll ring you today to see what your thoughts are.
>
> Best regards, Marc Smythe

Don't bluff! Only do this as a legitimate part of the end game of your job search. If you bluff and get caught, you'll look ridiculous.

NOTE: I have an excellent white paper on how to negotiate for salary on my website, www.donaldasher.com.

14

JOB CLUBS, CHANCE OPPORTUNITIES, AND PERSERVERANCE

Job Clubs

Why do people go to church, temple, mosque, or ashram? Because it reinforces and reinvigorates their faith, and puts them in touch with like-minded believers.

Why do weight-loss clubs work? Because once a week you have to show up and step on that scale, and that very fact keeps a dieter on track. No one wants to show up and say, publicly, "I did nothing," or worse, "I went backward on my goals; I gained weight."

Why do study groups work? They work for two reasons: students share their ideas about the content of the course and, even more important, it enforces that they will study for at least the length of the study-group meeting. On average, people in study groups score higher than people who study by themselves.

The same phenomena are in play for dissertation clubs. People in dissertation clubs have a higher rate of finishing the PhD than people who go it alone. It doesn't matter whether a scholar wants to be a PhD in engineering or in English—they can be in the same group. Knowing that you will have to show up every month or two weeks or whatever and tell others how your project is coming along is motivational for all the days in between.

Job clubs work the same way. Job clubs are proven successful. They can shave weeks off your search. **Join or start a job club today.**

If you have friends who are unemployed, meet once a week at someone's house; share the week's progress; discuss the coming week's goals. Read career books and give book reports. Share advice, ideas, leads, and referrals. Share horror stories from interviews. Help one another develop responses to nasty interview questions like "Tell me again why you were laid off?"

Job clubs can be formed around a level of employment ($100,000+ club), around an industry (high tech or health care), or simply around an area (Peoria). Some are even virtual. Many churches and some libraries sponsor job clubs. Run a search on "job club" plus the name of your city. The Forty Plus club, for professionals over forty, is active in many places in the country. Experience Unlimited is a job club run by the California Employment Development Department. Your state's employment department may run similar clubs. Most are free or charge small fees to cover expenses. If a group of people are laid off from the same organization, reach out to the people you like and admire to form your own job club. You don't need anyone's permission or sponsorship. Just do it.

If your job club uses this book as its guide, I will be happy to visit it or have a conference call with your group. This is a serious offer. The bigger your group the better. My phone is 415-543-7130, ext. 203, or drop me an email at don@donaldasher.com.

Chance Opportunities

This book advocates, strongly, for a well-thought-out job-search system. Plan your work and work your plan. However, there is another element in play that needs to be considered, and that is the huge part that chance plays in career development. You can have the world's best plan to be a high school soccer coach, and accidentally sit down in a park next to someone who works for the Olympics. You can have the world's best plan to be an accountant, and someone you meet at a party wants to start an education nonprofit.

Be sensitive to these types of opportunities. Explore them. Let chance push you around a little bit.

Have Friends or Be First; Be Patient or Change

In a tight market, jobs go to people with friends or people who get there first. If you'll notice, the HJM system is designed to get you in front of hiring authorities before a position is posted, or with friends on the inside who can vouch for you even if it has already been posted. It helps you find opportunity as well as beat the competition. It can even create opportunity. As you talk to hiring authorities and they see your skill set as valuable, they may decide to create a permanent position or a contingent engagement for you *even if they had no hiring plans prior to your contact.*

What this book cannot do, however, is create a job when there simply is not one out there in your market—at your level—for you—at this time. This is rarely the case, but for very highly paid workers, workers in industries in crisis, or all workers in areas of the country that are economically imploding, there just may not be a position for you in spite of your very best HJM efforts. If you fear that's the case, revisit the diagnostic tools for troubleshooting a job search. Make sure you are doing all you can to apply HJM techniques to your case.

First, follow this formula:

THE THREE TRUTHS OF A JOB SEARCH

1. You get jobs by talking to people.

2. You look for work in channels.

3. You need 100 leads at all times.

Review your search efforts on a weekly basis using the Sunday Night Scorecard on page 48.

Review the stages of a job search, and see if you can identify the source of the problem.

THE SEVEN STAGES OF A JOB SEARCH

1. Identify job targets (industry, function, title).

2. Identify raw leads (organizations, people, ideas).

3. Convert raw leads into lists of names of specific people.

4. Turn a name into an appointment.

5. Sell in the interview.

6. Stay alive through the selection process.

7. Close the deal.

The problem is almost always that the job seeker is not getting enough interviews. If you get enough interviews, you can do everything else poorly and still find a job.

If you decide that you are really doing all that you can do, and you are getting plenty of interviews and you're talking to people every single day, then there just may not be much opportunity out there. You can decide to wait for it to come back, or you can decide to change some aspect of your goal or process.

If you are a $400,000-a-year high-technology lawyer and no one is hiring lawyers like you right now, you're going to have to wait it out or switch your focus in the law or look at some of the law jobs changing hands at a lower level. If you are a $60-an-hour machinist and no one is hiring in your area at that range, then you're either going to have to take a pay cut or look in a more booming industry or more booming part of the country. If you're a renal transplant nurse and there's only one renal transplant unit in your area, you're going to have to look at another kind of nursing or another location. And obviously, if you've become discouraged in your search and are now looking for work six hours a week, the national average, then you've got to recharge your efforts.

The definition of insanity is to keep doing the same thing over and over again and expecting different results. This book is full of suggestions for activity. You'll try some and skip others, then go back and try again. Never forget that in the contemporary job market, you can take a job at reduced pay and responsibility *and keep right on looking for a better job*. The job market does ebb and flow, wax and wane. Even if you change nothing else, you can always recontact everyone every few weeks using the techniques in this book. Keep at it, one way or another, until you find what you are looking for. Try again. Try different. Try again. Try again. Try different. Try again.

You are worth it. All of society benefits when you contribute at your maximum desire to perform.

One Final Piece of Advice

See the facing page to read my one final piece of advice. If you fully embrace this truth, everything else will work out. Ultimately, this is the only thing you need to know. My best wishes for your continued success, now and in the future.

YOU GET JOBS BY TALKING TO PEOPLE.

INDEX

Printed in the United States
by Baker & Taylor Publisher Services

Printed in the United States
by Baker & Taylor Publisher Services